Business Development for Mom and Pop

How to Run, Develop and Grow a Small Family Business

By John P. Kuehn, Ph.D

Dedication:
   To the late Thomas O. Bardeen -
"Footprints in the Sand."

Table of Contents

11.   **Internet Advertising** - The Internet has been around for two decades. Initially, major corporations seemed indifferent, almost opposed to trying regular customer communication on the internet. Some, like the Yellow Pages wanted to pretend the Internet would go away. They sat back idly while Google became the dominant business search vehicle. Giant retailers worried that their investment in brick and mortar would be at risk if they promoted internet sales. All that has changed. All 500 top corporations now market on the internet, and most send out weekly or monthly internet "ads".

12.   **Web Site Design**- This chapter offers ideas and suggestions for making your website all that it can be. Years ago, the challenge was to persuade small business owners to take the time and invest a modest amount of resources in developing an initial website. Now, the challenge is to persuade small business owners to upgrade those start-up websites and make them professionally-designed marketing tools.

13.   **Social Networking** – The onslaught of social networking is revolutionizing the art and science of marketing. Facebook, for example, better be incorporated in to the website design as well as your overall marketing plan. Now, Facebook appears to be on the wane and you better consider Twitter, Pinterest and Instagram.

14.   **Organizational Charts** -   In the beginning the owner usually occupies most of the positions in the org chart. The objective is to have a different person in each position. They are not created around individual people, but rather around standard functions…. jobs or positions. People are hired to accomplish standard tasks, If someone leaves, they know exactly what position must be replaced. When you see yourself on the Organization Chart, you see who your boss is, you see what positions report to you and you see what jobs to shoot for in the future.

15. **Job Descriptions** - If a business plans to thrive and survive, all activities and procedures have to be recorded so they can be repeated and repeated correctly and efficiently. Also, someone has to be given responsibility for each of these activities. The organization charts tell us who reports to whom and once that is established, we can now define the responsibilities of each position.

16. **Action Plans** – Once Organizational Charts have been set up, and job descriptions are in place, your company is ready to implement Action Plans. The Action Plan System is the "heart" of the Business Development Program.

17. **Time Management and One-On-One Employee Meetings** – A regularly scheduled meeting....coffee or lunch meeting at the same time and day every week for thirty minutes between the team leader and each of the team members is both a very successful leadership technique as well as an extremely valuable time saving technique.

18. **Employee Discipline and Firing** - This is the core Action Plan in your Business Development Program. Every business owner asks: "How can I get my employees to follow the systems I am documenting?" This is the enforcement tool.

19. **Employee Hiring - The Recruiting Process** – Many small businesses are too casual in their hiring process. If you limit yourself to family members, acquaintances, friends, or even a sign in the window, you might get someone adequate for the job, but you will most likely not be attracting amazing people coming with experience from enterprises much larger or different than yours, ready to work for you with passion and creativity.

Chapter 1

Introduction

OK, if you're reading this you either own or about to start a small family business with less than ten employees.

I won't go into the statistical survival rates... I'm sure you've heard how bad the odds are. A huge number of businesses don't make it through the first year or two. It can take several years for a new business to initially get established and most do not have the capital to make it through the first year. They borrow enough to pay for the equipment and inventory, but they don't borrow enough for a year's worth of monthly bank payments or their personal expenses.

Then, when they start to get established, they are run by a jack-of-all-trades. Most people new to business.... multi-skilled workers... do it all... They plan, they manufacture, they market and they sell...they rarely get to spend. How many times have you heard: "I work 60 hours per week and make almost no money" ...There are a lot of businesses operating like this for years....tied to only one individual. When he/she dies or wants to sell, no one can take it over....no one would have a clue on how to run it.

The object of this book is to help you transform from a jack-of-all-trades to an entrepreneur. Eventually you will start working on rather than in the business and your work week should go down to about three or four hours..... I know, four hours, you see this and think how ridiculous that is, but think about it. How often do you see the owner of a McDonalds work at the store...or Starbucks... or any of the "successful" businesses???

Ben and Jerry's, Whole Foods, Wrigley, Mattel, Subway, Walmart, Macdonald's and KFC among many others all started out as Mom and Pop businesses. They didn't miraculously transform into large thriving corporations. They all had to adopt and follow the same principles and procedures large companies have been following for years.

If you're in school, just reading this book will make you familiar with some of the things you will need to do if you ever start a small business. If you're are going to start a business, you'll have a much better chance of survival by adopting the principles and procedures in this book and incorporating them in your business plan. If you are already a jack-of-all-trades, you will not be transformed by just reading the book and adopting a chapter here or there. It's sort of an all or nothing endeavor if you goal is to prosper.

Business Development involves continuous refining and redesigning a business in order to realize its full potential. It involves adjustments to management, financials, leadership, marketing, sales, information management, facilities, customer service and more. For a robust company able to withstand changes in the economic environment, business development never stops but is an ongoing process.

Unfortunately, many of the procedures and practices they use are not directly applicable to "small business". By the way, my definition of small business is under ten employees. Government has very few programs designed for the "small" retailer. Their programs are designed for "Small Business", but their definition of small business is gross sales of $5 million to $20 million. Their small businesses can have 500+ employees. Their research and programs are designed for these big guys.

The main thrust, goal and objective of this book is to provide a business development workbook for the small (under ten employees) retailer. Whether you're trying to break out of a plateau, or just trying to survive, the procedures, functions and activities explained in this book advance a small business from basic survival to a long term balanced growth mode.

   Each chapter is this book is designed as an individual project, but many chapters depend on projects completed in earlier chapters. You read the chapter and based on what you learned, you develop a plan of action for your business. Many of the chapters stand alone, but some sections, like marketing really need to be worked on in order. It's a ton of work, and maybe some expenses, but if you're a true entrepreneur you'll want the four hour work week. This frees you up to work on several "projects" at once. If you're a real entrepreneur you'll still put in a 60 hour week, but rarely will you spend more than a few hours a week on one of the "projects"

1. **Marketing.** Growing your business. You'll never be able to emerge from a worker to an entrepreneur until your business grows to a point where you can hire people to do all or part of your sixty hour work week.
   What color store interior makes men feel comfortable...what about women? What are your possible target markets and which should you shoot for and how. What form of advertising best works on your target market? What is the physical condition of your business? Do you need to remodel? Do you need to change

locations? How important is the motto or slogan? What is your USP (universal selling proposition)??? What about internet sites and...... and above all, don't downplay FACEBOOK and other social networks..... Social networking is free and we don't even know how far and in what direction it's going, but the effects on businesses are not ignorable....

2. **Operations Manual.** All of the day-to-day procedures, practices and operations should eventually be documented... Next Christmas you will look up the action plans for where the decorations are stored...what will be the advertising plan and budget? Which of last years ads worked? How many extra part-time people will you need and when should you hire them? What are their job descriptions??? What were the daily holiday sales statistics for the last few years? What was the answering machine message during the holidays? When you leave for a three day weekend what is the procedure for printing paychecks? What are the step-by-step instructions for giving a customer an estimate? Etc. Etc. Etc.

3. **Hiring.** When you need to hire a new employee to replace one who left, what is his or her job description??? What questions can you legally ask? What ads

do you run and for how long? How does a realistic hiring procedure work? How do you protect yourself from potential lawsuits? How do you train new employees?

4. **Organization Charts.** In the beginning YOU are probably every position on the org chart from CEO to bathroom cleaner. Your name is in every box. As you grow your business, you hire people that will take your place in given boxes. The long range goal is to have you in only one box. It also serves to show all employees who's in charge of whom...as well as what the openings are to shoot for...

5. **Dealing with employees.** Leadership. How to make sure the business runs smoothly whether you're there or not, hiring, firing, weekly meetings and the hidden values of such.

6. **Action Plans.** When an issue arises, the employee currently just goes to the boss and reports the problem. The boss makes a decision and tells the employee what to do. That procedure can take a half a day out of your important work. How many times during the day are you interrupted or bothered by employees asking you to solve every simple issue that comes up. We'll show you how to have your

employees solve their own problems and how to have systems in place to deal with all of the issues and unexpected problems that arise. Within a year or two of adding action plans as each unplanned situation is dealt with, you should be able to leave at any time without having to worry about the business being adversely affected.

7. **The computer**...... Are you one of the millions of intelligent people that say they don't want a smart phone or a computer because they don't want to be "bothered," when in reality they're really afraid they won't be able to figure it out... they're afraid they'll look stupid? I call them technophobes...You're not as stupid as you think... If a two year old can work his own iPhone apps you should be similarly able. How to remove the irrational fear of not being able to use it..... A smart phone as an every-day business tool is invaluable. If you're anti automation, your business will likely fail...or you will forever have to put in the 70 hours per week and carry around five pounds of post-it notes until you die.....You'll probably have reminder post-it notes in your casket.

8. **Inventory**......The nightmare decision of how much to have...how much to buy and when.....how to get rid of outdated inventory.....inventory vs. cash flow......inventory vs. profits

9. **Finance**...How many times has your accountant handed you the completed tax forms and revealed you owe the IRS.....usually on April 14th.... You look over the 1040 form and you wonder why the IRS accepts forms in Greek. Or, you have no cash flow, and the accountant tells you that you have to pay taxes since you made a profit. The accountant usually has no idea what you are doing wrong in your business, nor can anyone tell from the 1040 form... First we'll tell you how to hire an accountant...Then, we'll show you how to have two sets of books...one for the accountant and one that rearranges the same numbers so you can see a snapshot of your business performance on a day to day as well as in historical perspective.... You'll know well in advance whether you owe taxes and you'll know why your cash flow is where it is. You'll see what factors are being a drag on performance. You will be able to develop cash flow plans and projections that will allow you to sleep much more comfortably at night.

CHAPTER 2

The Operations Manual

OBJECTIVE:
To Develop an Instruction Manual for all Facets of the Business

I was reluctant to put this Chapter first because I was worried that if someone just bought the book and started here they would read the first two paragraphs and throw the book in the river. All you need from this Chapter initially is just to look at he categories and sub-categories to get a feel for what kinds of information you are going to collect and file in an Operations Manual. It could take years to fill in half of the categories.

The objective is for all activities regularly performed in the business to be eventually documented in as much detail as possible. When problems arise and an operation is changed or fixed, the documentation is changed. You keep copies of ads, commercials, letters to customers, and then later add comments on how they performed. You might want to re-use last year's Valentines Day ad if it performed well ... or you might want to change it based on last year's recommendations. With detailed job descriptions, new employees will be able to use the documentation to take advantage of the former employee's experience. When you occupy several boxes in the Organization Chart, and each of the boxes are documented, it will be easy to hire someone to take your place in a box.

It's not as bad as it looks. When you develop a policy or procedure, you write it down. It might be only one paragraph or sentence. You then save it in the right folder of the manual. Eventually, if you are undergoing a business development transformation, all systems will be documented and you'll be able hand the operations manual to the next CEO and he or she will have no problem taking over the reins.

Go through the categories below. I know it looks like a massive undertaking, but a little here and an entry there and eventually it will cover all the main every-day activities of the business. As you look this outline over, you'll say to yourself "Wouldn't it be nice if someone gave me theirs?" That only happens when you buy a franchise. They hand you the operations manual. Everything is there...its all documented. You can open up tomorrow.

Operations Manual

About the Company
1. Operations Manual Outline
2. Organization Charts
3. Company History
4. Mission Statement

5. Objectives
6. Other

Management
1. Company Wide Activities
2. Meetings
3. Usage of Time

Personnel
1. Employee Contracts
2. Employee Agreements
3. Employee Discipline
4. Employee Relations
5. Employee Benefits
6. Employment Laws
7. Hiring
8. Employee Leave Policy
9. Employee Meeting Policy
10. Sexual Harassment rules
11. Other Policies

Marketing
1. POS System
2. Advertising Slogan
3. Target Markets
4. USP
5. Marketing Budget
6. Website
7. Marketing Plan
8. Internet Marketing
9. Social Networking
10. Events
11. Advertising
12. Other

Financials
1. Chart of Accounts
2. Income Statement
3. Balance Sheet and financial ratios
4. Annual budget
5. Cash flow management system
6. Sales and credit card procedures
7. Collections process
8. Purchasing
9. Inventory control
10. Payroll
11. Other

Daily Operations and Procedures
1. Telephone procedures and scripts
2. Computer and Internet Usage
3. Product Delivery Systems
4. Service Delivery Systems
5. Action Plan Systems

Facilities
1. Building Legal Agreements
2. Building Maintenance
3. Building Space Allocations

Some examples of items you include in your operations manual:
1. Employee job descriptions for each position
2. Action plans for production procedures: a problem might have developed in making hamburgers....the raw hamburgers were left out too long after being taken out of the freezer.

The action plan was to install a smaller refrigerator just adjacent to the grill so they would stay cool until they were cooked and be accessible.

3. The recipes for all of the food items, where to buy them, etc.
4. Telephone answering machine messages... a special message for Christmas or for a vacation, etc.
5. Purchase order forms
6. The equipment acquisition process – Ex. In order for a new piece of equipment to be ordered, there are five steps…. A listing and explanation of each of the steps would be entered into the operations manual under the appropriate category. When someone specifies a need for a new item of equipment, he or she can go to the operations manual and look this up.
7. Action plans for finance/administration
8. The weekly employee meeting procedure
9. Thank you card designs and procedures
10. The company organization charts
11. Office supplies maintenance and inventory procedure

The categories above are very general. There are many more possible categories. And there is no formal classification system as yet. As the Manual grows with the Company, it will be necessary to organize the categories in a logical manner and give each category a classification number. The larger the company, the more information will accumulate. Each entry will eventually be given a classification number so that the information will be easily identified and located.

It seems like a lot of material to prepare if you're just starting your business. It might take a year or more to fill in all the necessary steps, but after that is accomplished you will be able to work on your business rather than in it. Before an operations manual is completed, the owner has to run, manage, work in and work on the business. How many business owners have you heard complaining they work 60 hours per week working in their business???? How many owners of McDonalds have you heard say that?

The operations manual allows the delegation of authority. Of course a lot of Mom and Pop businesses are situations where Mom and Pop are both the managers and the workers, but as growth takes place, delegation will start to be instituted.

Chapter 3

Target Markets

First An Overview of Marketing

Marketing is concerned with all the principles and procedures you use to convince the public to buy your product or service. I will cover how to choose a target market; the importance of an advertising slogan and a statement of why your company (product) is better than anyone else's. I will also discuss the business name, logo, signage, store design; the importance of merchandising; dealing with your customer clientele and the customer experience; how to advertise; and then web design and social networking.

If your goal is to save your business, the best way to do that is to grow your business. The best way to do that is to undergo a business development program. Just fixing your advertising, for example, will not be productive if the customer experience is mediocre. Advertising is also pointless if you are not targeting the right customer. My point is, to do it right you're going to have to go all the way. Half way will probably just postpone your premature retirement.

I recommend you read through all of the marketing chapters and then go back to each one as a workbook. Choose your target, develop a slogan...a logo... put it all together for your business and then you'll have a chance to bring it all to the next level.

Target Markets

Market researchers have historically looked at demographics to choose their target markets. Higher income buyers buy different products at different prices than middle incomes, etc. This is what has been historically taught in college marketing courses. But, corporate marketing researchers have found that different personality types behave differently within similar income groups. For example, extroverts behave differently than introverts when it comes to buying decisions. They've also looked at different occupations for isolating differences in buying practices....psychographics.

It's mostly agreed that purchase decisions are made primarily from the "unconscious mind", sensitive as much to the "experience" as the "product". Some people are persuaded primarily by "price", but that's just about 1/3 of the market. Call these "DEAL PEOPLE". The quality of the item is not as relevant as price. It's all about the deal or perceived price. They'll spend $10 in gas traveling to five different stores searching for the best deal. They shop for general merchandise almost exclusively at Walmart. Over the years, my most aggravating and stress creating deal customers have been used car salesmen, or worse, car dealership owners who started out as salesmen. They want to pay you less than half of the marked price and then they want you to throw in a two pairs of matching items as well as a free trip to the Bahamas. On the other hand, try to get a deal on a car you want to buy from them. As my business program progressed, we stopped advertising to this target.

Another group will "pay more for more". That's another 1/3 of the market. They look for quality but they want it at the best price they can get. They investigate all the attributes of the product and try to get the best features at the best price. Call these "QUALITY SEEKERS".

A third group, another 1/3 of the market is nearly "price insensitive". This group demands "emotional gratification" and lots of attention. They want to know they're getting the best...the most unique. Call these "PRESTIGE PEOPLE". They want the best of the best, as long as they can afford it. And it's all about the experience.

These three groups are not sensitive to incomes. Very rich people can still be Deal People, and low income people can still want the best or the most unique... as long as its in their budget.

Most of us will fall under one of these three categories...or at least a weighted combination of two of these categories depending on the product. I should also emphasize that it's also possible that for one product someone can be a Deal Person and for another they can look for Prestige. Harley Davidson marketers are experts on this. Again, none of us behaves just one way under every set of circumstances. However, most of us will behave in one of these three ways, most of the time. Understanding this is highly valuable to savvy businesses. You can't be all things to all people. If you are pushing low price, you will get customers looking for low price (e.g. Walmart). If you are supplying the best, you will get customers looking for perfection whatever the price. You must be out of your mind if you think you can satisfy both of these customers with the same product!

Now, before you jump all over this, it is an obvious simplification of the nature of people's buying habits. There are many combinations and cross sections of these three types of buyers, and those combinations and interactions take up a lot of the thinking processes of marketing "experts". You, on the other hand can't afford to hire marketing "experts", and you can't afford to invest in the extensive research, which sometimes narrows the target for their company's product. Also, you will never have an advertising budget large enough to experiment with the types of ads that work on a particular segment of interest. You are stuck with variations of the three groups above, or maybe some weighted combinations of the three. As long as you see the logic of the three groups, you will be able to direct your marketing plan.

The truth is that a very large number of businesses worldwide misguidedly try to satisfy everyone. They advertise that their products and services are the most diverse, the prettiest, the most intuitive, the very best, yet they are magically the most affordable and cheapest at the same time. Most ads generated by small businesses fall on deaf ears, because they are promising all things to all people, and that doesn't attract serious buying attention.

Marketing is where the large companies have a serious advantage over the small businesses. They have marketing staffs and big budgets for marketing research. The big advantage, however, is being able to test the marketing. Large companies spend millions testing their advertising slogans, their logos, the effects of certain ads on sales, among other things. For example, Geico. First, its cave men, then a stack of dollar bills riding a motorcycle, men living under rocks, an intelligent pig and making mistakes building the pyramids. We all know about the gecko. I'm sure they know the quantitative effect of each, even though it looks chaotic. It looks like they can't make up their minds on a theme. I'm sure they are measuring different segments of different targets in different geographic areas at different times of the year.

The large companies are also able to differentiate their products for different targets. The auto companies do it with different models...the Corvette vs. Vega vs. the Silverado, for example. It can also be done with the same product of different qualities. Diamonds, for example, can be sold in top qualities with unique mountings top prestige buyers and poor quality stones in inexpensive mountings can be marketed to deal seekers. I see new restaurants open selling hamburgers or hot dogs for a dollar or two each. They'll beat everyone in town. However, I wouldn't bet I could beat MacDonald's... Why not open an exclusive shop? Sell a super hot dog, one foot long, with a pound of chili and condiments and an order of french fries that no two Sumo wrestlers could finish in a week. Sell that for $10. or $15. The more exclusive or unique or impressive, the higher the price.....the higher the profit margin. You've chosen a different target. A caveat on this: If you are a restaurant selling cheap hot dogs, just adding the "Big Dog" to you menu might not work. You have to change your appearance and advertising (your marketing plan) to attract the "Big Dog" customer.

Your Market Research Manager (You) must do the leg work. If you have an existing product who are your best customers? What do they like to hear and see, and how do you fulfill their needs? If you are a start-up business, you have a super advantage. You can design your product and service and your venue to attract and satisfy the target you choose. The first and most important function is to determine which "segment" of your Customer Database loves you the most and which segment would you love the most to attract.

It's interesting to note that high end prestige companies have significantly higher gross margins than Walmart. You have to attract a much higher volume of customers to pay your expenses when your price margins are under 10 percent. The higher end companies have fewer customers that spend more.

In my personal experience, I was originally catering to DEAL PEOPLE and some QUALITY SEEKERS. I advertised lowest prices in town. My gross margin was approaching negative. The changes I instituted were many and varied. The main marketing change was to un-target DEAL PEOPLE and to concentrate on PRESTIGE BUYERS. A very effective tool in this targeting was to adopt an advertising slogan...

Chapter 4

The Advertising Slogan

This chapter unveils a subtle but extremely powerful marketing tool. At first, you might think it's a waste of time, but pretty much all of the major corporations worldwide follow this modern marketing principle. Are any of them wrong? Can you afford not to follow their lead.

Harley Davidson – American by Birth. Rebel by Choice.
Volkswagen – Think Small.
Porsche – There is no substitute.
Aston Martin – Power, beauty and soul.
Walmart – Save Money. Live Better.
Reebok – I am what I am.
Nike – Just do it..
Calvin Klein – Between love and madness lies obsession.
Marks & Spencer – The customer is always and completely right!
Levis – Quality never goes out of style.
Tag Heuer – Success. It's a Mind Game.
3M – Innovation.
IBM – Solutions for a smart planet.
Sony – Make Believe.
IMAX – Think big.

DuPont – The miracles of science.
Energizer – Keeps going and going and going.
PlayStation – Live in your world. Play in ours.
EA – Challenge everything.
Blogger – Push button publishing.
Canon – See what we mean.
Nikon – At the heart of the image.
Kodak – Share moments. Share life.
Olympus – Your vision. Our future.
FedEx – When there is no tomorrow.
Red Cross – The greatest tragedy is indifference.
Disneyland – The happiest place on earth.
Holiday Inn – Pleasing people the world over.
Hallmark – When you care enough to send the very best.
Fortune – For the men incharge of change.
Ajax – Stronger than dirt.
Yellow Pages – Let your fingers do the walking.
McDonalds – I'm loving it.
KFC – Finger lickin' good.
Burger King – Have it your way.
Coca Cola – Twist the cap to refreshment.
M&Ms – Melts in your mouth, not in your hands.
Nokia – Connecting people.
Vodafone – Make the most of now.
Coca Cola – Open Happiness.

Attributes of an Advertising Slogan

Once you get an effective slogan, it helps cut through all the advertising noise to get your attention. They are an accurate representation of what you do. They build your brand identity. They set the company apart from it's competitors. Consumers retain the right slogan, they associate your business with it. It makes them believe your product is reliable and desirable.   And, it gives them a good feeling about the company.

One example and probably the strongest advertising slogan of all time was "A Diamond is Forever"....... DeBeers. DeBeers was basically the manufacturer, and distributer of diamonds. They were the only distributor at the time. They were a benevolent monopoly. They started using the slogan in 1947 and it inspired unprecedented growth in the jewelry industry. It's interesting that it was also pioneering as a wholesaler advertising to the public, so its retailers would have to carry more diamonds.

Another example of an advertising slogan creating a growth machine is Avis. "We're only number two, but we try harder". That slogan propelled them from mediocre to a real strong number two. Wendy's was a mediocre MacDonald's competitor until a little old lady, presumably at MacDonald's asked "Where's the Beef?" The rest is history.

You have to be old to remember this one, but Clairol (Hair Dye): "Does she or doesn't she?" It brought them from mediocrity to major. And finally:

JUST DO IT!
The slogan was coined in 1988 at a meeting of Nike's ad agency Wieden and Kennedy and a group of Nike employees. Dan Weiden, speaking admiringly of Nike's can-do attitude, reportedly said, "You Nike guys, you just do it." The rest, as they

say, is (advertising) history. The "Just do it" slogan has become and still is considered to be one of the most influential and inspirational in the history of branding. And you might notice that almost every time you see the slogan, you see the logo. In fact, now when you see the logo, you thing Nike and you think Just Do It. That's what you want to do for your business. Start brainstorming.

Will a slogan work this well for your company? Probably not, since you don't often come up with the slogan of slogans. But, once you determine the profile you want to target, and you come up with a slogan that will attract their attention, you have a start. Many companies change their slogans. They test them out over time and if they're not happy, they develop a new one and try that one out.

I hope by now you realize that you cannot afford to ignore the use of an advertising slogan. Even if it's not earth shattering, if the public associates your business with the slogan, they will think of your business when they see it. It has to be everywhere in your marketing handbook....on your business cards, as you answer the telephone, on your letterhead, on your signage, in your radio commercials, on your website, on the baseball shirts of the little league team you sponsor.

How to create your own slogan
Creating your own slogan will take some brainstorming. First try making a list of all words that describe your product. It might help to use a thesaurus. Add synonyms. Add the store name to the list. (Assuming you already have a name. If

you're just starting a business, it might pay to use your slogan as the name). Then make a list of the attributes and benefits of the product. Then you need to have a session with short combinations of these words. It could help to have two or three people with you. Each will come out with some combination of the listed words and the others will comment. It would help to have one of your friends who "annoys" you with bad puns. You know who I mean. That person, could be of great help. It could take several sessions to come up with some alternatives. Then you can test them with customers. Social networking is a great way to perform such tests.

If you don't come up with anything with this technique, there are dozens of Internet sites that call themselves advertising slogan generators. Some are free. If you still have no luck, it might pay to seek a professional company. I'm not personally familiar with any affordable such companies. You might want to search around. Make sure if you find one that you check out their references. Get some samples of successful slogans they developed.
Good Luck!

Chapter 5

Unique Selling Proposition
USP

Your advertising slogan can often make the sale, or at least get the customer in the door. And, it should get them in the door with a positive buying attitude. The slogan takes effect the instant they see it in an ad, or when they hear it when you answer the phone (very important).

The Unique Selling proposition is a more detailed slogan. It defines what makes your product and your business better than those of your competitors. Why should you buy from us rather than them? An ideal USP explains there are no other products. There are no other businesses.

OK, who is your customer? By now you have chosen the customer you want. You know your customer. You have chosen your target. That customer is not buying your product. He or she has a problem.... buying your product solves that problem. Cosmetics companies, for example, don't sell cold cream, they sell style, class, glamour, confidence. Your USP shows how you and only you solve their problem. A paint store doesn't sell paint. They sell a beautiful wall, a new fresh look for your bedroom. A jeweler doesn't sell engagement rings. He sells the look on a girls face when her boyfriend puts the ring on her finger. What are you selling to a woman in a fine shoe store? A commercial can just show a beautiful model walking up the street with a classy pair of shoes. The problem is that customer doesn't look like that model. When she buys the shoes, problem solved.....

In a restaurant, you're not buying dinner, you're buying an experience. You're socializing with friends. You are meeting new people. You're being made to feel special....important. You're showing off your new outfit....how well you look dressed up. Remember, the Julia Roberts movie "Pretty Woman"? Richard Gere wanted her to have a great experience buying new clothes. He wanted the sales people to suck up to her. It wasn't the clothes, it was the experience. What did that clothing store sell?

When you buy a gift for someone's wedding, are you buying something practical and useful? No, you want that gift to be a message from you to them. That message could be many things. I spent a lot, so I care. You'll never forget this came from me. I don't much care, so here's a saltshaker. So, the question to the gift shop owner is how to show your customers you can help them send the right message.

Problem: I have to get this package delivered tomorrow or I'll be in trouble.

Solution: When it absolutely has to be there overnight – Fedex

Problem: When you need to sell your house in a hurry without losing money
Solution: Simms Realty's five step process guarantees your house will be sold in two weeks or there will be no commission

Problem: The kids are starving but Mom and Dad are too tired to cook
Solution: Pizza Delivered in 30 minutes or its Free - Dominoes

The USP therefore serves as the skeleton of all your advertising. Your ads show your customer's problem. (The customer doesn't always know they have a problem.) You then show them what they look like after their problem is solved.

A huge percentage of big company advertising uses this same format. Watch some TV ads. Listen to the radio. Look at magazines. Look at billboards. The advertiser first mentions a frustration or anxiety, then offers some relief to that frustration or anxiety.

Now, the challenge is to implant the solution to the problem into every aspect of your sales process. Your Company Slogan should be everywhere. It is on your Business Card, on your Letterhead, Stationery, in your E-Mail, and in all your Advertising. A simple rule is that if there is time and space, you should always show or state both your Slogan and your USP. If not, you go with your Slogan and your Company Name.

   Your USP won't "fit" everywhere your shorter Slogan appears. However, it commonly appears in Telephone Answering Scripts, on Web Sites, Internet Ads, Company Brochures, and Monthly Internet Newsletters. Also potentially on Radio and TV, your USP will constitute the basis of the commercials.

On our jewelry website under "About Us":

At Kuehn Sisters Diamonds
we understand and appreciate your
concerns and frustrations. Are you
making the right choice? Will it fail
to impress her? Is it the brightest and the best?

Kuehn Sisters' diamonds and fine jewelry are
selected specifically for their ability to
startle and dazzle. We take the simplest
and convert it to the unique. Our personal
service system and quality standards are designed
to completely alleviate your doubts and fears.

Chapter 6

Branding and Your Image

The American Marketing Association (AMA) defines a brand as a "name, term, sign, symbol or design, or a combination of them intended to identify the goods and services of one seller or group of sellers and to differentiate them from those of other sellers." Therefore it makes sense to understand that branding is not only about getting your target market to choose you over the competition, but it is about getting your target market to see you as the only one that provides a solution to their problem.

We have discussed the Company Slogan and the Unique Selling Proposition and they form the heart of your brand. And as we have discussed, you must integrate these tools and statements and strategies throughout the company at every point that you come in contact with the public. It is the objective of this branding process to present an image, a picture, a sense of your company that when a potential client comes in contact with your brand they get a sympathetic feeling for you... they like you, they trust you, they want to deal with you... It's not so much your product, but something in your image that intrigues them.

Your Logo

Your logo is only one piece of your branding strategy. It's a symbol that can provide your potential clients with instant recognition of your business. Your public must be familiar with your slogan and your USP and ideally they will see the logo every time they see the slogan and/or the USP. Once they make the connection, all they need to see is the logo and they will associate it with your business... your brand... your image.

Characteristics of a Good Logo:

1. It should boost your company recognition. It should enhance admiration, create trust, be memorable.

2. It should communicate strength and integrity.

3. It should be simple, not busy or complicated. It shouldn't have too many fonts.

4. It should be different from others especially your competitors

5. If your company has a color scheme (and it should), the logo should incorporate those colors. Not too many colors, and not too

busy. And the logo should not rely on colors.
There will be many instances where it will
have to be black and white, such as in the
newspaper.

6. It has to look good both large and small.
Remember the different media where you
will be using it.

If you are designing it yourself:

1. Decide whether to incorporate the company
name. It has to be distinctive rather than
generic.

2. Don't let it look amateurish. You might need
professional help. Avoid stock art or trendy
designs.

3. Make sure you are designing it for your
target, not yourself. You don't have to like it if
it accomplishes your objectives.

4. Create multiple designs and test them. Try to
get feedback from your target market. Get
opinions on social media... You might use a
social media contest to get opinions

Your Business Name

If you have an established business, it might pay to keep your name, especially if you have an established clientele. If you are totally rebranding your business, you might want to change it. An ideal name would be the same as your Company Slogan... Not an easy task. If you keep your name and change your brand, it can work, but you have a lot of work to do. It happened with Ebay and Amazon and a lot of the big online companies, but it would have been easier to start a company with a name that implied its business.

It sometimes helps to use your own name as the company name. The risks are that all of your "good" customers will want to see just you. They will shy away from your sales staff. This will make vacations hard to come by, although MacDonald's, Colonel Sanders Wendy's and many others managed to get away with it.

Sometimes it can be an advantage to invent a person's name for a business. If you have an Italian restaurant, you probably don't want to name it O'Reilly's. On the other hand, that might be a memorable name for an Italian restaurant that could catch on. There is a restaurant in my town that's called The Dirty Bird. One of my rules is never use the name "Dirty" in any part of a restaurant's name. However, this restaurant has the best fried chicken that I have ever had, and I'm a regular customer. It's always busy and apparently the name had no negative effects. They also have something quite unique; fried chicken and waffles.

It brings your cholesterol up to 1000, but I'll go to the gym tomorrow morning. Now, if you are saying to yourself that you'd like to try that restaurant based on what I just said, then you might realize that I need to write another book on just restaurants. Just my word of mouth has convinced you to try their food. (I could be an accessory to murder by cholesterol). Their market fulfillment system accomplished the mission of the slogan, the USP, and the Logo. It created the Brand. If you are selling jewelry, or clothing or gifts, or almost any product, you will be very lucky if you can accomplish what The Dirty Bird did. The downside is the owners (husband and wife) are there all the time. They do all the cooking, all the waiting on customers and all of the other assorted chores. Although they have one or two kitchen helpers, they need the rest of this book to find out how to go from sixty hours per week down to three or four.

SIGNAGE

You will discover as you learn about advertising that the store sign is probably the most productive means of advertising your business. Ideally it should be visible to a large number of passersby. It's your cheapest form of advertising because once it's installed there is no monthly fee. Since many people who have never heard about you may see the sign, it's important the sign attracts their interest. It should also convey your brand. It should not be too glitzy if you are trying for a dignified image. It should be memorable and noticeable.

In many locations you are prevented from using certain sign designs. In Malls, for example there are strict limitations on color and size. Similar limitations occur in many downtowns. These laws were designed to prohibit "objectionable" signs. The trouble when Government makes these laws is they often go overboard on restrictions. It could pay to get creative with the Company Name if you are prevented from other means of displaying your brand.

If you can do it with class, it could pay to use your name, your logo and your slogan on a sign. If you have developed productive versions of these tools, putting them on your store sign could significantly increase your store traffic.

Store Facade Design

The importance of the façade goes without saying. It's obvious it will be advantageous to have a store façade that conveys your brand along with the sign. This is a real tough area, because very few business owners are in a position to change the façade. Ideally it should blend and complement the sign. Also, it should fit with your brand if possible.

It could be very expensive to change the façade, and if you are renting, it would depend on the Landlord. There could be instances where it would pay to move locations. For example, you could be a fine jewelry store located in a building with cheap looking store façade. Neighbors could also be a problem. The stores on either side might detract from your image.

Interior Design and Merchandising

There is a science to the interior design of a store. Supermarkets analyze walking patterns and they strategically place merchandise to maximize walk-by sales. They put the most in demand items such as milk and eggs as far from the entrance as possible. You have to go past a series of items specifically designed to attract walk-by attention. You didn't go to the supermarket to buy these items, but now that you see them, and in attractive, intriguing packaging, you realize how much you need them.

Most of the foot traffic in a jewelry store is repair customers, so they put the repair department in the back of the store. Customers have to pass the showcases to get to the repair department. Similar strategies are used in many retail stores.

What are your store colors? Do they make your customers comfortable? Research has found men are more comfortable in any shade of blue. Women are comfortable in any shade of red. Do you have carpet or hardwood floors? Which goes better with your image or your brand?

If you have found ways to get customers to walk by your merchandise display, you must use some science to display or merchandise your products. I recommend you go online and search for the best ways to merchandise your products. Look how your competitors do it. Better yet, visit the big stores that carry your kind of merchandise. Visit the stores you want yours to look like in the future. How do they display items? In jewelry, the experts recommend you only have four or five items per linear foot of showcase. Too much inventory packed together does not attract your interest. Then you need to display them on risers in clusters of matching rings, pendants and earrings. In clothing they display dress shirts and matching ties next to the suits that are on sale.

The Customer Experience

Now that your marketing plan has attracted a ton of customers into your store, what are you going to do with them? If they are not impressed the way they are welcomed they'll tell you they're just looking and will find a way to leave as soon as they can. When they walk in the door they will get an immediate impression of your business. If it's negative, they're out of there. Things like the music that is playing or the aromas they smell can affect their decision to buy or leave. It would be beneficial to research the music your customers would like to hear in the background, and how loud they would like it. Avoid playing your personal preferences if you find your target likes something else. Aromas are also more important than you think. Research has found that if you provide the right aroma, customers will feel welcome. And, when they encounter that same aroma elsewhere, they will immediately think of your store.

Some businesses are too dark or too bright. Some restaurants are so dark in an effort to create an ambiance, that you can't see the menu...... or the food, when you get it.

Then there is the dilemma of the way you greet your customers. I remember years ago in my Mall store, a lady came in the store around a corner, so she didn't see me standing there. When I started walking towards her (I was behind the counter) she started backing away.... without making eye contact. Just because I'm sometimes obstinate I went towards her faster. She backed away faster and basically ran backwards out of the store. Mall customers are in a different category than downtown street customers. They don't want you near them until they are ready to see something up close. They are extremely frightened of a fast talking, high pressure salesperson. A lot of them are just wasting time on a Saturday night and have no intention of buying anything. They get tired of telling salespeople they're just looking. Notice what the big box stores do. Among other things they have big screen TV's on the counters showing commercials and product information.

There are countless companies that train you to sell. One thing they all tell you is never ask the question "Can I help You?". Also never ask "What can I do for you?". They recommend you mention the weather, or a local event or that's a real cool shirt..... You get a conversation going and you wait for the customer's body language to change and then you can ask what they want. Another thing you can do is have something unique in a showcase, and as your talking about the weather you can ask if they think this item is cool. They also recommend your staff wear the jewelry or clothing or other items you sell. In a restaurant, it can add to the experience if you give the customers a "free" sample taste of your special of the day as they are waiting to be seated or as they are seated and reading the menus. Once I had a restaurant owner offer me a taste of something and to my surprise, it was on the check. He lost my family's business and everyone else I told about the incident

Think of ways you can impact the customer's opinion of you as they walk in your front door. That opinion will often be the deciding factor of whether you make a sale and more importantly whether they will come back. I think it was a Huddle House in Georgia that really impressed me because basically everyone in the restaurant loudly said "Howdy!" when my family walked in the door. We always remembered that and since then we always look for a Huddle House when we're on the road.

A Note on This Chapter

OK, so, in this Chapter, I haven't given you any useable cut and dried concrete answers. But I have given you a homework assignment. You need to go through each of the categories in this Chapter, do some research, ask some questions and think of ways to make each of these the best they can be. You know you've done the right thing when you overhear customers leaving your shop using the expression "Wow, that place was cool". (I should mention that you won't get that response from young people, but you will get Facebook and Twitter comments.)

Workbook Projects
  1. Your Business Logo
  2. Business Name
  3. Store Sign
  4. Store Façade
  5. Interior Design
  6. Store Color Scheme
  7. Merchandising
  8. Aroma
  9. Music
  10. The Overall Customer Experience

Chapter 7

Engaging Your Customers

Note: If you are not computer literate and you don't carry a smart phone, go to Chapter 10 now. Do not start this Chapter if you haven't read and embraced the enlightenment of Chapter 10.

A Point of Sale Computer System.

If you don't have one, you need one. Research has found that business increases 25 percent when you keep in contact with your past customers. These systems have been very expensive in the past, but now are becoming more affordable because you can get cloud systems for a monthly fee. They work on any computer with a user name and password and the data are stored in the parent company's servers…. the cloud, if you wish.

The first thing you get is a customer's contact information. I have found that it is extremely easy to collect customer information when you imply that it is necessary to take this information for every sale or transaction. I have found almost no reluctance for customers to supply full addresses and phones. Email addresses become easy when you offer warrantees where you ask the customer if they would rather be notified by phone or email . They are also less apt to refuse emails when you tell them they'll be getting special flyers or coupons. I now find an increasing number of customers that want to be notified by text. We often hear customers say they didn't get the phone message or the email, but they always get the text message. We also get the spouse's name when appropriate and we collect birthdays and anniversaries ...wish list information if you're in the retail business. It rarely hurts to have too much information.

Along with the contact information, you will also have a record of everything the customer bought and when and how much he spent. It will show the inventory number, which tells you the manufacturer of the item, the size and the cost of the item. This comes in handy if the customer later wants a matching ring to the pendant for example.

There are countless valuable reports, such as sales by category, inventory cost of sales by category (gross margin), sales by manufacturer, fastest moving items and many other related reports. There is a Jewelry POS program called The Edge. They take information from all of their member jewelers and are able to show some very valuable information to the members. Most valuable is a table that shows hundreds of manufacturers. They list the major items sold by each of the manufacturers by stock number. It shows how many jewelers bought the item and how fast it sold. You can then see which manufacturer sells more items faster and it's price range. I assume similar POS systems are available for many retail products. If your industry doesn't have such a POS company, you have a business opportunity.

How to Keep your Customers Coming Back -- ---Clienteling

I've mentioned before that keeping in touch and engaging your customers can increase your income by 25 percent. Can you afford to ignore this resource? Different businesses handle this in different ways, but the main idea is to find ways to convince your previous customers to come back to the store and while they are there, find ways to show and sell them more merchandise.

In the jewelry business I never paid much attention to clienteling, but recently, after prodding from Sherry Smith of the Edge Retail Academy I developed a system that we (my daughters and I) are putting into operation. Historically, when we sell a ring, we automatically replace stones that fall out at no charge to the customer, even years down the road. Also, if we repair an item and that item breaks again in the same place, we also take care of that at no charge. I figured that since we do this anyway, why not give the customers a free warrantee. So, with each new item we sell, we give them a "free" three-year warrantee certificate. The catch is the customer is required to bring in that item every six months for inspection, or the warrantee is void. We also give them a one-year free repair warrantee with the same six-month inspection requirement.

OK, so they come in every six months, what do you do then? We place wish list forms on all the counters and also Hint Hint Cards. When a customer comes in for an inspection the staff is trained to ask them if they want to fill out a wish list for their next occasion. We offer to help them pick out the right piece and on the form, we add the finger or neck size along with the model number and price of an item. Then there is a place on the form for us to add the spouse or potential gift giver's phone or email address. We offer to text or email him that the occasion is coming up and we have a wish list that will solve his problem of what to buy for her occasion. If she doesn't think it will work to call, email or text him, we have Hint-Hint Cards. The item will be described on the card. It has our logo on it and all she has to do is set the card on her dining room table with the noticeable Hint Hint in plain site.

Sherry suggested our sales people all wear the latest new merchandise that recently came in so they approach the warrantee inspection customers and show them the latest new styles. Along with that, our showcases have to look inviting and intriguing so the inspection customer will notice items as they walk by. Small TV screens with our commercials and videos of some of our special merchandise could also help our clienteling efforts.

Now, there are many different retail store owners reading this book..... Your assignment for this Chapter is to come up with a plan that will get your customers back in the store, and what to do with them when they do come in. Keep in mind many shops are clienteling with ipads and mobile phones. They have ipads in strategic locations where customers can fill in their own wishlists, or they are entering their contact information, etc. The technology is changing and evolving so fast, that when you come up with a new use for a phone or iPad, it's already being done ..... and then there are new apps being developed daily.

Events and Mailings

A very good method of bringing your customers back into the store is to hold events. There are countless possible themes for in-store events. They can be as simple as ladies night out, trunk shows where manufacturers bring in their new items. You can have external events such as charity benefit dinners or even benefit golf tournaments. Some of these will bring people to the store to buy, and others develop your positive image.

Once you have a customer list and records on their purchases, you can invite all customers that spent more than $100 or $500 in the last year. You can invite them to preview showings (and sales) of new items. You can mail your repair customers a letter reminding them to come in to have that item inspected. There are countless ways to get old customers back into the store. But, is your store merchandised to the extent that when you get a large number of old customers back in the store, they will easily notice and buy something? Will they be impressed with your new inventory? Will they be excited enough to recommend their friends.

Greeting and Salesmanship

Greeting the customer the right way can make or break a sale and all future sales. The question is how to do it right. I mentioned that in malls, the customers live in fear of sales people. They don't want to be greeted until they are absolutely ready to buy. I found the only approach was to say "Hi" to everyone as they walked in. If they kept eye contact with me I would start a conversation.....the weather, sports or current events. If they avoided eye contact, I would say to them "If you want to see something let me know" and I would leave them alone until I saw them stop at a particular showcase. Then I would approach them and pull something out of that case and tell them a story about it. That would hopefully lead to the piece they were really wanted.

Greetings vary depending on the situation. If a couple comes in shopping you might greet them differently than you would a single person, for example. Almost all retail products have a national organization, or private enterprises like The Edge Retail Academy for the Jewelry Business. They will have salesmanship programs among others. If you are having difficulty in this area I strongly recommend you contact the appropriate organization for your industry. Have them train you and/or your sales staff. And, see what they have to offer for areas other than sales. But, above all never say "Can I help you."

Do you pay your sales staff on commission? There are many, many opinions on this subject. There's no definitive answer. If you pay 100 percent on commission you'll tend to have hard sellers and cut-throat competition among staffers. If you pay no commission, you could have a staff that just puts in their time. I feel a happy medium is salary plus commission. A practical way to do this is not to base the commission on that salesman's sales but on the stores sales. And furthermore, a more practical way to do that is to base the commission on the store's net income rather than sales. Using that technique motivates employees to find ways to cut costs as well as increase sales.

Answering the Phone

Remember in Chapter 4 that you need an Advertising Slogan. One of the most important functions where you use the slogan is when you answer the phone. It will not be easy, but you should "force" your staff to answer the phone using that slogan. They will resist, because it sounds hokey. But a new customer can be convinced he or she is going to buy from you just by hearing the slogan ....the right slogan.... when you answer the phone.

An example: "Smith Clothing Emporium where we make you look your best. This is John speaking". I know it sounds like a little much, but it can really pay off. Try calling some of your big box competitors. See if they use their slogan. If they answer their phone with an automated press one for service, etc. you will have a real advantage. First of all a human answers and then the first thing they say tries to solve your problem and alleviate your fears. It convinces them they are calling the right place.

Schmoozing

The Urban Dictionary defines schmoozing as: *Making ingratiating small talk – talk that is business oriented, designed to both provide and solicit personal information but avoids overt pitching. Most often an artifact of "networking." It is more art than science but can be learned.*

I have witnessed the lack of schmoozing cause businesses to fail. I see this most often in restaurants. Think about it. What makes you go back to a restaurant? New restaurants open up and they have great food, great prices, and a nice atmosphere. You go there and are very satisfied. But, you never really feel like going back. You give the place a positive word of mouth recommendation, but only when you are asked. Why don't you go back? What happens in your favorite restaurants that beckons you to come back?

You frequent a restaurant and other businesses more often when the owner or manager, or other employees make you feel special. They appreciate you. They ask you about your kids. Where did you go on vacation? They call you up and tell you they're getting in an order of fresh fish on Thursday. They greet you by name. They are genuinely glad to see you when you come in. The owner sits down with you and schmoozes for a few minutes and then he or she does the same for other tables. He brings you a sample of a new dish they are creating and asks for your honest opinion. You return to this restaurant once a week and you recommend it to everyone, even if you are not asked.

If you have a business other than a restaurant, schmoosing is just as important. A business should make you feel like one of the family. Have a coffee dispenser and a sit-down area in your store. In some situations it doesn't hurt to have a bottle of something stronger under the counter. Your business needs a personality. Your customers want to hear of your latest personal exploits. They like to hear stories and see the pictures.... in the store and on Facebook or Instagram.

Schmoozing is absolutely necessary for business development, but it can lead to problems I try to cure in this book. If the owner is the chief schmoozer, then everyone that comes in wants to see him. He's much busier due to the business development program, but he's now a full time schmoozer. For some people that's fun, but my goal for the business owner is a three or four hour workweek. So, don't put all the eggs in his basket. Train your sales staff to schmooze. Each should have a customer book. They should have the contact information of all their customers along with their personal data such as: they have two children, Doris and Jeff. Their mother Helen lives in Montana, the husband is a fireman and they have a dog named Spike. Of course now that's all on an iPad rather than a note book. And, a good POS program will have space for this type of information. You enter it right after the customer leaves.

Dress Code

In my early days in the jewelry store, I dressed casually. I didn't want to appear stuck up. However, when I discussed dress with Tom Bardeen, I got an interesting question. He asked " If you were searching for and interviewing a potential new accountant or banker and he or she came out of their office to greet you wearing a T shirt with their logo on it, would you be impressed?"

I wore a suit every day since he asked that question. I required employees to wear suits and our image, I believe, was strengthened. Also, there was never a dress down Friday. A dress down day implies a dress down in service. What would you think if you went to a funeral on a Friday and the Funeral Director was wearing jeans?

Of course, every business is different, but consider the message you send to new customers with the outfit you are wearing. I have very few young people stopping in the store dropping off resumes in the last ten years. In the 1980's and 90's, I had an average if two or three people a week. Lately, its once a year. I had a young man come in the store a few months ago with a resume. I was surprised, since he was the first unsolicited applicant I had in over a year. And guess what he was wearing. Yes, jeans with the crotch hanging slightly above the knees. OK, he was about 17, so he might not have thought his outfit could affect people's opinions of him. I wanted to sit down with him and educate him a little. At least he was looking for a part-time job. We will discuss more on Millenials in other Chapters.

Chapter 8

Inventory Management

This chapter will probably be the least valuable of all the chapters in the book. The reason is that nothing concerning inventory management is cut and dried.... There is no workable science. That's because all businesses are different and the rules for one do not work for another.

The ideal inventory management situation only occurs when you have a company that sells one product in one size. There is only one wholesaler that produces this product and it's always available immediately and is always the same quality, the same price and the same delivery charge. This company would know that it sells exactly ten of these every day, seven days per week and customers are indifferent as to which one they buy. This company only has to stock 70 of these items and will have a standing order to deliver 70 new ones once per week. This company resides in La La Land ..... All companies in the real world have varying levels of scientific management and most of them use a lot of guesses.

Most companies selling inventory offer a selection of shapes and sizes. They'll sell more of one size than another.... they sell more in one shape than another.... they sell more at certain times of the year than others. How many of each size should they ideally stock and when? How many different but related products should they carry? They have to find the best supplier...one that has good prices, one that will deliver immediately, one that supplies the best quality and the most saleable designs. They want a wholesaler who will provide merchandising materials such as fliers and display apparatus and advertising co-op. There are companies that make their own inventory. How many and what sizes should they make?

They say the more turns in inventory you make the better. So, if you have $50,000 in inventory and you gross $1,000,000 in a year, that's very good. If you have $50,000 in inventory and you only gross $10,000 in a year, that's very bad. If you're not sure how much in sales you're going to generate in a year, its difficult to estimate how much inventory to stock. Most companies stock more than they need and their profits are reduced accordingly. If you're just starting up a new business, it's probably a good idea to have more stock than you need. It will give your customers a positive impression. If you have almost nothing in stock, customers tend not to come back ..... you don't have a selection. As your business matures, you can manage inventory to achieve more turns by restocking fast sellers and reducing if not eliminating slow sellers.

A useful system for some companies that sell a myriad of products seasonally is the following:

	Jan			Feb		
	Purch	Sold	change	Purch	Sold	Change
CATEGORY 1						
CATEGORY 2						
CATEGORY 3						
CATEGORY 4						
CATEGORY 5						
Etc.						
Totals						

This table can give you some insight as to how much you're buying and selling of each product, each month. And you can summarize this with the following table:

Month	Purchases	Sold	Change
Jan			
Feb			
Mar			
Etc.			
Totals			

If you set this up with an Excel Spread Sheet you might use the two charts to analyze and plan your buying of inventory. If you have a comprehensive POS program it should be able to print out reports such as these with all of your products' categories.

Inventory Vs. Profit Vs. Cash Flow

How does inventory relate to profit and cash flow? The obvious answer is the more inventory you sell, the higher your profit ..... derr. On your income statement is a category called cost of goods sold. This is a calculation accountants use to determine your net profit...your taxable income.

Very simply, your profit is determined by taking total sales, and subtracting cost of goods sold (The total amount you spent on the inventory you sold) and then subtracting your expenses. Cost of goods is an intricate accounting procedure because it is a function of the amounts you spend on inventory and the amount of inventory you sell or don't sell.   The simplest way to describe the formula is over a certain time period it is calculated by adding total purchases of inventory to the dollar amount of inventory at the beginning of the period minus the dollar amount of inventory at the end of the period. This little accounting action is often the reason why you don't have cash flow and don't know why. It explains why you think you're losing money and your accountant tells you that you made money. The reason, you make a profit and have no cash flow is you can't deduct the cost of goods you don't sell.

Case 1 –Assume your total sales are $100,000 in a given year:
During that year you purchase $50,000. worth of inventory. The inventory on hand at the beginning of the year is $75,000 and at the end it is $65,000. Cost of goods is:
Purchases $50,000 Plus Beginning Inventory $75000. minus ending inventory $65,000 = $60,000.

Your cost of goods sold is $60,000.   And your gross profit (before expenses) is $40,000.

Case 2 –Assume again your total sales are $100,000.

During that year you also purchase $50,000. worth of inventory. The dollar value in the beginning is also $75,000 but at the end it is $85,000. Your cost of goods sold is $40,000. And in this case your gross profit is $60,000.

This is what happens often in businesses. In both cases you grossed $100,000. Assuming your expenses were the same to sell $100,000 worth of goods, you have the same amount of cash available at the end of the year. However, you made much more money on paper in case 2 than in case 1, because your gross profit was much higher. You might have had a higher mark-up in case 2. The product mix you purchased in case 2 could have been more efficient. Knowing these figures is going to now allow you to analyze how your profits are derived. What did you buy in Case 2 differently than in Case 1.

Goals

What kind of inventory should you carry??? Remember you chose a target market. Do you have the items that target wants. If you're targeting price buyers, stock items you can discount. If you're targeting prestige buyers, stock impressive, unique items. If your goal is to increase a certain category of buyers, have more items in stock in that category and fewer of the category you don't want to increase.

If you want and expect to increase business next year don't just increase your inventory budget by five or ten percent. You might want to carry higher profit items with the same inventory outlay. You might want to change your marketing strategy. One rule of inventory I've found is if you want to sell two or three of a certain item, you must stock ten or fifteen of them. If you just carry three of an item in hopes of selling those three items, you'll probably wind up eating them.   The overall object is to use as little inventory as possible to generate enough total sales to cover your expenses plus. And, stock the kind of inventory you don't have to discount.

Some Strategies and General Rules

In the jewelry business, salesmen come to your door to peddle their wares. One of their favorite slogans is you can't sell what you don't have. That's true, but if you buy everything they have and overstock your store, you will wind up with a ton of merchandise in your store that hasn't sold in years.

Some general guidelines:

Reorder the fast selling items immediately. Get as high a markup as possible on the fast sellers. Mark down the slow sellers....or scrap them if possible

If an item hasn't sold in a year or in a reasonable amount of time after a markdown ..... scrap it for whatever you can get. It's costing you money otherwise. Let's say you have an item in stock that costs you $10.00 and you sell for $20. It hasn't sold during your normal inventory turn...three times per year. You could have sold three of these for a total profit of $30. So not selling this $10 cost item in a year cost you $30.... If you discount it to $10 or even $5 you would be ahead if you used that scrap money towards something that will turn three times.

Software

It's very important to have software to keep track of your inventory. It will allow you to develop strategies to grow your business. And it will enable you to analyze trends and swings in your business. If you're in retail, a POS program (Point of Sale) is a necessary tool. If you're running a business without one you're never going to grow. It will allow you to keep track of your inventory on a daily basis and programs are available in most industries. A point of sale program takes the customer's personal data, keeps historical records of that customers purchases, enters each transaction as it is made....takes the item out of inventory as it is sold, and enters the sale into your accounting system all in one operation. Then it will print out various reports such as the one mentioned above. It will show present and comparative sales figures and the kind of information you need for decision making at all levels of organization. It will summarize the items you sell which should aid your decisions to replace fast moving inventory and isolate inventory that needs to be scrapped.

An interesting note is there are organizations in certain industries that will tabulate sales of member businesses. If they have enough members they can tell individual members what products are selling.... who manufactures them.... Their average revenue and more. If your industry doesn't have this information, you might find a profitable business opportunity here. How much would you pay for such information.

Apologies

I said at the beginning of this Chapter that it wasn't going to be a lot of help. Hopefully I've given some guidelines, but I've never been able to find a definitive solution to inventory management. If any reader has an unbeatable system, please contact me and together we'll make millions marketing this to the masses.

Chapter 9

Advertising

As you undoubtedly know by now, marketing is much more than just advertising. In fact, many marketing "experts" downplay the importance of advertising. Advertising naturally flows out of a good marketing plan. However, the major objective of any small business is to make a profit. Eventually the idea is to attract customers. If you have an effective integrated marketing plan, advertising is logical but still not simple. It is essential to use the Advertising Slogan and the USP in your advertising to attract the segment of the market you've targeted. The question is how to reach your target market in the most cost effective way.

Remember we have three main types of buyers. If you want to attract the price buyers, advertise sale, sale, sale, 20% off, 30% off etc. 90% off, etc. We'll beat everybody's price, now and forever. If you are targeting quality bargain buyers, mention features and how you're supplying the best ones at the lowest prices. Example: Our cars have the best safety record because we have the best antilock brakes at the lowest prices in town. If you're targeting prestige buyers, advertise you have the best of the best of the best .... because you're worth it...or she's worth it... Use your slogan and USP statement consistently.

Millennials

I need to add an addendum to the three psychographic segments and it involves Millennials or Gen Y's. They range in age from 18 to 32 and the marketing world is in a tizzy about them. I've heard dozens of generalizations about them. They are waiting longer to get married. They are waiting longer to get a job. Two factors affect this: The job market is terrible for recent college graduates and many Millennials are not awfully serious about getting a job. Their ideal jobs do not exist right out of college. I say to them facetiously they want to start out at $200,000. per year with a 25 hour work week and six weeks of vacation.....twice a year. There is also something new I see with this group, and that is they feel four years of college was very rough and tiring, so before they start a job search, they need a vacation. There is one very interesting thing about them, however, and that is a very large number of them want to become entrepreneurs.

Now, the reason I bring up Millennials is I'm told by the big marketing gurus that the millennials do not fall in any of the psychographic segments. They're in a category by themselves. Nobody is really sure what motivates them to buy a particular product. I believe they will eventually have to fall into one of the three main segments, but they have to do a little maturing... and they have to start making a living.

I'm doing some informal surveys of our Millennials customers to try to get a feel for how to market to them. I surveyed a sample of my customers in the jewelry store to see what they do at night after work. They get into bed with a laptop in their lap, an iPad on their right and their phone on their left. Very few have regular TV's. They watch TV on their laptops. They study or read or do social media on their tablets and they text on their phones. They do this for three to six hours a night. OK, where to you place ads to attract their attention?

My plan is to put some commercials on Laptop On-Demand cable TV. Yes you can do that now. Another part of my plan is billboards. They do eventually get out and drive somewhere and they'll have to see a billboard. They do not usually read the newspaper. Their total source of news is Facebook (Scary, I know). Facebook is on the decline as of this writing. It's for "old people". Now I see growth in Pinterest and Instagram. The question is now what message can you use that will bring them in your door.

I'm still using romance, although I'm told by the Gurus that Millennials do not respond like their predecessors. They like funny…. They like outrageous. They like high tech. They also like causes. They are generous contributors to causes and advertising your cause can attract their interest.

I'm afraid that if you need this demographic, you are going to have to do a lot of trial and error advertising. The big retailers have a big advantage because they have a large marketing budget and staff. See how the big guys in your industry do it and try your own version of it.

I talked to a girl (in her early 20's) who needed a shovel for her garden. She bought it on Amazon. I asked her how she knew it was the best shovel for her needs. Why didn't she go to a local retailer and ask them what the best tool is for their problem. She said the shovel she picked got good reviews and she spent a total of two minutes ordering and it will be delivered to her house tomorrow. She didn't have to waste a lot of time driving to the store and dealing with some salesperson. You might want to examine potential market fulfillment systems that will attract this girl. Lot's of luck!!!!!

A note about having sales

If you target the price conscious deal buyers, you must use sales. A problem that arises is that they won't walk in the door if there is no big sale going on. In some areas there are rules against permanent sales. Many department stores suffer from this syndrome. They even have a calendar in the marketing manager's office. One week shoes are on sale, the next week it's perfume and lingerie. Other problems arise with pricing. Most retailers that are sale oriented must have higher retail prices so that they can make a decent margin when they sell an item for 50+ percent off. Their target market is the most likely to comparison shop and they aren't happy when they discover the prices were raised for sale purposes. The key, if you wish to follow this path, is to brand your merchandise. Make it unique or give it the illusion of being unique. An example is the Nike insignia or the alligator logo on sport shirts. You associate those logos with quality, so a sale means something. It might be noted, however, that these two companies have branded so well they rarely need sales.

Where do you place your ads?

If you're targeting price buyers, advertise in the media that price shoppers read, watch or listen to..... the free newspaper vs. the daily paid paper. Younger shoppers however rarely read the newspaper. If you are looking for younger shoppers, you might advertise on the rock radio stations rather than the oldies stations...... However, recently there is a trend away from commercial radio to internet radio. Advertise on Pandora. Then there is Facebook and Twitter and now Pinterest and Instagram..... and tomorrow ten new online and mobile sources. Your market cuts across all income levels and ages, so you want to reach the most people per dollar while your aiming your particular message toward your target.

The worst way to advertise is to wait for the media reps to approach you with deals. They'll have specials and all will be "bargains". The best procedure is to first set up a budget. If you're a start-up you should estimate your year's income and pick a percentage.... In the beginning it could be 8 to 10 percent... established businesses are often around 5%. But if you want to grow and get established, you'll need slightly higher budget. Then, don't wait for the reps. Call each one and make an appointment. Make them work for you. Have them bring their ratings...their statistics. You want to know how many people watch, listen to or read that media so you can determine cost per "impression". How many people are in your target? You want to know who they are. They should know about psychographics. If they don't have information on who their audience is, or how many there are, you might want to reduce your budget for that particular media.

Once you've established a budget, now you can make up a plan. In that you must consider timing and seasonality. If you sell Halloween costumes, don't advertise them in May. Set up your advertising plan for the next year in advance so that it maximizes the number of impressions per dollar of your   budget. You have to plan your advertising around sales, promotions, events, holidays and shows in advance. Then, as you are using the various media try to document the results. If you get a lot of comments on a particular commercial on a particular station, place that information in the Operations Manual. As you get more and more feedback you will learn where to concentrate your resources.

In your store, have a sheet of paper entitled "What brought you into the store?" Have a row for TV, Radio, Billboard, Website, Newspaper, Facebook, etc. After a few weeks to a month, you should be getting some useable information.

There are several schools of thought on how to advertise.. an important one is TOMA-- Top Of Mind Awareness. That involves getting your name out there every week.... Smith Jewelers----When it has to be Unique, for example. Then, no matter when a guy needs and engagement ring, the name will be fresh on his mind. The other school of thought is that all advertising should pay for itself.... Bring in the coupon....or buy one and get the second one free, or 30% off all in-stock merchandise. They compare the cost of the ad campaign with the amount of revenue you bring in You must realize by now there is no definitive answer. Different products respond differently to the various forms of ads. The big companies have a marketing department which analyzes the possible approaches. They test a particular ad campaign in a particular market and use the results to determine their best action. Small businesses have to trial and error it. Although, if you have a large mailing list, you can test out a promotion on a small sample and if it works, send it to everyone.

TV Cable has some advantages over newspaper and radio. They usually have extensive research on their audience, and you have some logical types of choices. Wealthier people tend to watch the travel channels.   But, remember if you are looking for prestige buyers, they go across all income levels. Some channels tend to attract certain types of buyers. Prestige buyers, for example, tend to watch the food, travel or romance channels. There are also some products that are better advertised on TV than newspaper. Moving visuals can be very powerful. TV advertising, however, is often more expensive than newspaper, per impression. Cable TV stations usually have lower rates but they are based on the number of people who watch.

Your least expensive form of advertising is sometimes better than all of the others combined.....Your store sign! If you are in a high traffic location (if not, you might think about the cost/benefit of moving) your sign should be visible to a ton of people. In this case, the name becomes a very important commodity. If you can, it might pay to make your name the same as your Company Slogan. (Chapter 4) The name should intrigue your potential customers' interest. Your logo also is important here.

Don't forget your own customer database. It has been estimated that keeping in contact with your own customers will increase your gross by 25%. For example you can send a gift coupon to your best 1000 customers. Or you can contact everyone that spent more than $250 in your business in the last three years. I ran an interesting campaign once that sent my thousand best customers two gift cards. One was for them, and the other was packaged as a gift they could give to anyone they chose. When they presented the gift card, they had to tell the recipient how good a store we are.

Things to consider when making up ads:
    1. Keep it simple...not too much clutter
    2. Send the message to your target----prestige buyers need emotion for example

3. Provide information.... the customer has a problem, you have the solution, anxiety - anxiety relief, from your USP

4. Show them your product is better...the best.... The best of the best

5. Your ad should be different. The most important part of the ad is how it stands out from the competition...does it attract one's attention?

6. Your eyes should immediately see that ad when surrounded by other ads

7. It should also be unique when presented on the radio or TV. What will prevent the viewer from flicking it off.

Not easy..........????? No it isn't..... Bigger businesses have a marketing department. In new small businesses, the owner needs to be a Jack-of-all-trades, so he or she is also the marketing director. It can sometimes pay to hire a marketing or advertising agency. There are also now a number of organizations online who provide ads and campaigns that can work for you. Hopefully from this book you're learning to ask the right questions.

Social Media Advertising. There is a huge amount of potential. Certain businesses will benefit more than others. You have to be very careful not to irritate your target. Don't put a commercial in front of a video you're sharing, for example. It's better to be informational. Engage your friends, followers, fans. Ask questions....Get a dialog going. Create a buzz or a controversy. It's so far, fairly inexpensive, so it might be an advantage to pay for more friends.

This is an area, where it would be a great help to see what the experts are saying about social media advertising. Again, I recommend the Dummies Books.

Chapter 10

IT – Information Technology

O.K. Some of you will be able to skip this Chapter after the first few paragraphs. The rest better read this and heed.....in fact, even if you think you don't need this Chapter, I advise you to read it.... You'll have employees who you'll need to train.

Every day I hear from intelligent people: "I don't bother with computers or Smart Phones.... I don't have time for them". There are many variations but the theme is the same. I call you people TECHNOPHOBES. A technophobe is a very intelligent person who is so intimidated by technology that they cast it off and don't want to "bother" with it. Actually they're afraid that they will look stupid if they can't figure it out..... it's only for young people... If you're reading this, you are, or are about to run your own business. Are you not smarter than a ten year old???? A twenty one year old????? I have a two year old grandson that can take his mother's iPhone, turn it on, find YouTube and play movies... Since he can't read, he doesn't always get the movie he wants, but he figured out how to start them and stop them as well as search for them. Is he "smarter" than you technophobes???? He still wears diapers!!!!!!!

I'm aware of the problem because I was an actual victim of this intimidation. I started working with computers in grad school in 1964. I did research using main frame computers and then bought one of the first desk tops, the Radio Shack Model II for my business use. I learned on my own how to use DOS and could actually work the only three software programs in existence that came with it. I learned to program in several programming languages. Then years later, Windows and the Internet appeared. I thought at that time there is nothing valuable ever going to come of the Internet. It didn't do anything practical and I never thought it would ever come to anything.

Then, one day I was visiting friends and their 15 year old son was working on his "Windows" desktop. I walked past his room while he was doing something on the machine. First I saw this screen just full of little faces and pictures (icons they now call them.) I had no idea what I was looking at or what any of them were. There were dozens of them, they were all different and even with my glasses, I couldn't make out what they were. Then he clicked on one of them and started clicking and clicking at lightning speed.... window after window. The screen was flashing faster than I can blink. He kept clicking and zooming and flashing and I was never able to see what he was actually clicking on. Before I could read three words, he was on the next set of window screens. Talk about intimidation.... That kid appeared to be thinking at a rate faster than the speed of light. I slinked out of there and quickly decided that was too complicated, too massive an undertaking for me... It was devastating that anyone could actually think that fast. I was too old to ever figure that out.

It was five years later that my DOS computer crashed ..... Judgment day... I had to have my customer list, my accounting program, my word processor.... What was I going to do? No more DOS available anywhere. This was during the early 90's I believe. O.K. I took the plunge and ordered a new machine...with Windows.... I opened the box and followed all of the instructions to the letter. Then, no matter what I tried I couldn't get the thing to turn on... The instructions were not written by a novice. They were written by someone who had done it so often, they assumed you knew to include three steps that didn't bear mentioning. That's what I thought, but I later found out they were written originally in Chinese and they were translated in India.... Once I got it turned on, I didn't know what to press....nothing made sense. The instructions were worthless. I got on the phone and made five calls to NY and finally found someone with a manual...a step by step guide to Windows. (Now I use the Dummy's books)

Aha!!! I read the manual cover to cover before I went near the computer. Then I re-read the manual with hands on the computer, and as I read it, I went from step one all the way up to just barely getting by with the basics. The funny thing is my screen now is filled with Icons and I appear to go from screen to screen at lightning speed ..... to the uniformed. In reality, as you go from screen to screen, you know what to look for and where to look. You know where the window or box is going to be and you press the box just as it comes up. You appear to be thinking at this lightning speed. Computer geeks love to do this in front of normal people. They love creating technophobes.

Another incident involves my son-in-law the computer engineer. He was modifying a picture of a car with Adobe Photoshop and I was looking over his shoulder. I asked him why he didn't turn the bumper into chrome. He said you can't do that because chrome isn't available in the color pallet. I said "Give me ten minutes". They went into the kitchen for a drink and when they returned the bumper was chrome. He asked how I knew that. I leered at him and triumphantly said "I READ THE *"XXXXXing"* MANUAL!!!!!!!!!!"

Therein lies the problem. Most of today's software comes with little or no instructions. The young kids won't read a manual even if there was one… "We don't need a manual". Old people have a lot of trouble with that. With no manual you're afraid to press the wrong button. When you do get there, you're not sure how you got there…and forget about getting there again.

Young people appear to pick it all up fast. But in reality there are similar patterns and layouts in the workings and layout of most software. After you get the gist of the patterns you can more easily pick up the new applications. As a result the younger people can operate the programs relatively quickly, but until they read the manual they're not going to be able to create chrome. To me that makes the future scary.

Anyway, my answer is get the Dummy's book.....There are also Idiot's Guides. Most of them go from how to turn it on to a step-by-step guide as to how it works. You read the book and work the thing and after a while you'll be able to operate the thing. You'll be able to show your two year old grandson which movies he's not supposed to watch on YouTube. You'll be able to get a movie of your granddaughter dancing via email from out-of-town in the blink of and eye

THE SMART PHONE

When smart phones came out I jumped on them. I had mastered Windows, now I can't wait for new technological advances that make life easier and more fun. I originally used Blackberries because that was for the "sophisticated" business user. But, Apple was an innovator and the iPhone offered everything the Blackberry had plus a lot more. Anyway, I'm going to show you how easy it is to operate and show some of the ways it makes your business easier to run.

Note: I hate the name smart phone. We need a new name. The fact that it's a phone is incidental. How about a "datacom"?

Some Apps that are Simple and Practical:

1. If you press the photos icon, you'll get several albums worth of pictures. I not only take fun family pictures but I take pictures of my renters' drivers licenses, a necklace someone is wearing, or ring's I see somewhere that I want to show someone. I showed a customer an intricate gold chain she wanted to get her daughter. She didn't want to buy it until her daughter saw it and liked it. I took a picture of the chain on the mother's neck. The mother called the daughter in California while I texted it to the daughter's smart phone and she loved it. This whole procedure took less than a minute and the lady bought the $3000 necklace...did it pay me to have a smart phone?

2. The camera is really high quality. I didn't remember how many megapixels, so, as I'm typing this, I got my iPhone out, pressed the Google (g) Icon, then pressed the small microphone symbol and spoke into the iphone the following: "megapixels iphone 5 camera". A dozen websites popped up informing me it's an eight megapixel camera. You can take still pictures or movies and save them for future use or email them to friends ... email them to your desktop, etc.

3. The Weather. Anywhere you press that, you get the current statistics, radar, and a five day forecast. There are a thousand weather sites you can choose from. My most important use for that icon is on the golf course. If you hear thunder in the distance, you check the radar and see if it's coming your way. I always walk the golf course and one day when I saw a major storm on the radar, I called the clubhouse and had someone drive out to where I was and managed to get back just in time. The technophobes were dodging lightning and running for cover. I did pick up one on the way in.

4. Keeper is an App (Application) that stores all your sensitive information. It's encrypted and even the best geeks can't get in...so they say. I keep all my user names, passwords, safe combinations, etc. All I have to remember is one password to get into Keeper. By the way, this, along will all the rest of the information on the iPhone is backed up on my desktop and everything on my desktop is backed up in the cloud. I use Carbonite. Every night it backs up everything. For those of you who back up manually on an external drive, my advice is to forget it. It's one thing if your hard drive blows...but what happens in a theft or fire. With Carbonite, I can go to Montana, buy a new desktop, download everything on my

now burned up hard drive....but that's a password I keep in other locations.

5. Logmein. One of the main reasons I went to the iPhone. (Blackberry didn't have it). It's a remote control program. You enter a user name and password and you get your office desktop on the screen. You can then operate that desktop from anywhere in the world that has Internet access. I can write paychecks to the printer in my office if I'm out of town. I also check and answer certain email when I'm not at the office. The screen is much smaller, but there's a lot of piece of mind.

6. The calendar. I make entries in it every day. I schedule a meeting for Thursday at two and even have it ring me a reminder message an hour before and a day before. It enters the date on my desktop computer and on my laptop at the same time. If I'm at my office I get reminded on my phone and my desktop at the same time. If a colleague or employee needs to go with you, they can be added as an "invitee". Then the appointment is sent to the invitee's calendar and miraculously it appears.

7. Contacts. I had about 500 business contacts on my desktop when I got my iphone and was able to download all of them. I add new ones as they come up and sync them with my desktop. You can search through them, call them, email

them, text them, enter any notes about them you want to remember later and you can send and receive contacts via text and email. I recently got a new laptop for home use. I use it for writing this book. When I first turned it on the night I got it, I was asked for my iCloud password. Then by magic all of my contacts, all of my photos, all of my appointments and among other things all of my bookmarked websites appeared when I downloaded Google Chrome.

8. You see the Facebook icon and I know what you're thinking. Don't judge Facebook as a social network. Keep in mind there are more than 500,000,000 members. What advertising medium do you use that come anywhere near that? I check Facebook (two or three minutes) twice a day and will go into detail in Chapter 31. Open up your mindset for this one.

9. Simplenote. My office desk used to consist of two dozen separate piles of notes. There were ten or twelve different categories. I specialized in 4 x 6" plain sheets. I bought them by the case. I used to make notes to remind me to look at another pile of notes. My desk now is almost clear...just one pile of papers...and the only reason I have this pile is that there were no categories I could figure out...... Simplenote allows me to create categories. Then notes are typed under each category. It's easy to add notes

and easy to delete them. I'm able to check through my notes several times a day to see what I have to do next or remember what to do soon. There is another use for this App for you entrepreneurs out there. If you require your key employees to have iPhones (you'll probably have to buy them), each can download the Simplenote App and each can log in with the same username and password. Then you can have categories for each of them to share...tasks for certain of them to do. Each will see everyone else's tasks. When you add a note, the same note is added to all the users. Other users can add notes to your categories, etc. They sync automatically. When you delete one, that one deletes on all the phones...it leaves some interesting possibilities.

10. Textalert Plus. This is a very handy little App. Tomorrow I have to be at a meeting at 11:00 am. Or I want to remind my wife that she needs to be at that meeting also. If I remind her today, there's no guarantee, but if I remind her twenty minutes before the meeting, life is good. You type in a message and schedule the time it's delivered. It works for any phone that receives text messages.

11. Messages. That brings up texting, and interesting phenomenon. I'm not sure why it's so valuable a means of communication. It's easy to get a message to someone

without having to worry about interrupting them or putting pressure on them to answer right away. It's the only way I ever communicate to my student renters. College students never answer their phones (they all have smart phones)…. they never admit whether or not they get email and will never respond to email…but they unfailingly respond immediately to a text even if they're in class. I also have Group Texts ….. If I want to tell all my renters they have to stop partying after 3:00 am. I can get this to all of them in one message.

12. Email. I'm going to assume that most of my readers know what email is. However, I've found it a very valuable tool in a different way. I'm getting out of the shower and I want to remember to call someone. I email from my phone to my desktop. When I'm at meetings, I take notes and email them to my desktop. When I get back to the office, all of these reminders are there. I delete them as I accomplish them or transfer them to the appropriate locations.

13. Dragon Dictation. This one makes texting easy. You press the Dragon Icon and say a message into the phone. It's converted into text and asks you if you want to email or text it to someone. It's great for one of you old people who can't remember how to type. And for iPhone users there is Siri. You press the Siri button and she will text for you or email or call someone. She will

read emails and texts to you when you're driving. And, she will answer many questions. For example, I was playing golf during a West Virginia University basketball game. Wanting to know the score, I asked Siri: What's the score of the WVU vs. Kansas Basketball game. She told me the current score and how many minutes were left.

There are thousands of other business uses for the iPhone... You can take a picture of a document and actually fax it to someone. I use the thesaurus a lot. You don't have to buy a GPS for your car. You can search Ebay with the Ebay App. You can play any kind of music you can think of at the same time you're doing all this other stuff. You can use any of 289 different calculators. You can use voice memos. Press the App, say what you want to say and keep it on file. You can use any one of fifty different alarm clock apps, and you can read any of 25,000 eBooks ..... (Note: I read the eBooks on my iPad... I can make the print large enough to read without glasses)

In the beginning it's basically a phone, but once you get in the groove...follow the directions...read the Dummy's book...a monster will be created. Hopefully from what I've shown you here, you'll realize the value of the tool... a tool you'll need if you want to keep ahead of the coming new wave....

One last note: I didn't want to sound like I'm selling iPhones. There are a ton of other phones out there. Most of them are cheaper than the iPhone. Many of the techies get Android phones for various reasons..

you can program them....they're cheaper...but the iPhone is the benchmark. All the others are compared to the iPhone. I don't recommend any specific phone in this book, but I used the iPhone as an example for purposes of explaining the value and need for smart phones in business. You might also realize that when it comes to technology, I'm a Prestige Buyer. I want the best. I don't want copies. The Attribute Buyers will buy the less expensive Androids and Deal Buyers will try to find ways to get out of using a smart phone. When they have to have one, they will look for the cheapest version available.

Chapter 11

Internet Advertising

Keeping in Contact with your Customers

It's hard to measure, but it goes without saying that not keeping in contact with your customers can lose many of them. It's also logical that keeping in contact can make you money. These are people who have bought something from you in the past. You spend advertising money trying to get strangers to come to your store. Your former customers have already been there. Which group will be easier to sell?

People who start small businesses are shy about contacting their customers. They worry about aggravating their customers by joining the list of companies that bombard them with junk mail. This attitude is the result of being themselves bombarded by emails, phone calls and First Class letters and magazines by every company you have ever bought from. We usually delete these emails and throw away the letters and magazines without reading them at all. It's not particularly bothersome, but it's in many cases a waste of time and energy. If your customers don't hear from you, however, they can become indifferent and lose any loyalty they may have had. I guess there can be an argument that it's better to send an email that gets deleted than not to send anything.

Email Newsletters

Almost all companies will find a way to get your email address and send you newsletters. If you are the right customer, you might be interested in the content of some of these. Some send coupons and sale announcements. Others send information on new products and services. The goal for a small business is to identify your clientele and send them something interesting or intriguing. It will remind them of your existence and maybe prompt them to revisit your business. Even if they delete the newsletter, they will be reminded of your existence.

Website Ads

Some websites bring in as much revenue as the company is making by selling their products. If the website has a ton of volume for whatever reason, they can sell banner ads and make a lucrative income. YouTube makes a huge amount of income by selling ad space on their high volume videos. The owners of the videos make money on these ads. Depending on your business, you might want to advertise on one of these media.

Another offshoot of banner advertising is fascinating in it's development of a unique idea. When someone visits your site for whatever reason, the site places a cookie on the visitor's computer. Then, as that person visits other sites that are larger volume sellers of banner ads, your banner ad opens on that site. So if someone visits your site and then they go to ESPN for example, they will see your banner ad on ESPN. There are hundreds of sites like ESPN that are members of this network. If they click on your banner ad you pay $1.00. You give the company a budget and when it reaches that amount, people will stop seeing your banner.

If you have a retail store, it's not clear that you will gain customers by having people visit your website. However, a growing number of retail stores are adding E-Commerce to their websites if they are selling unique items. Customers see the item for sale on your website and may stop in the store to see the item. There is also the option of selling it online as do the big box stores.

Sponsored Links

Again if you are not selling unique items online, attracting people to your website may not prove to be a valuable investment. I have found, however, that almost no new customer stops in a store without first going to the website. For that reason it's important to have an engaging website.

If you feel that attracting traffic to your website will be valuable, then sponsored links can be very valuable. When you search Google, you see sponsored links on the top of the page and on the right side of the page. These links show up when certain key words are entered. You pay a fee for these if they are clicked. There are free tutorials at Google for these. They are a little complicated, but doable with some persistence.

Note: An interesting side note. You can now sell your merchandise on Amazon and you can advertise your products on Amazon. It's not expensive. If you have a product that is unique, it might pay to look into Amazon's tutorial.

Chapter 12

Website Design

With the emergence of the internet, it became more obvious every day that businesses needed a web presence. Early websites were one page with a picture of the sales staff standing behind the counter. Businesses put a print ad on the front page, gave their contact information and that was it. Even today we see sites like that. Do they, in any way, motivate you to go to that establishment? The original purpose was to get you the phone number and open hours schedule. That still is one of the most common usages.

Now, the buying public demands much more than a picture of the sales staff saying "we provide the best service". In fact, at the point we're at now, almost no new customer will visit your establishment without first visiting your website. If you don't have a website, you don't exist. Keeping that in mind, what do you want your website to tell these new visitors? What do you want your target market to think of your business when and if they visit the website? What should they see when they first click on your site? Remember, the average length of time one spends on the landing page is about 6 seconds.

Features a Website Should have

Well, lucky for you to be reading this book. You know the answer to that question. The first thing they should see is your brand. You've been working on that in the previous chapters. They should see your logo and your slogan first. Your USP can be expanded and put in the "About Us" window.

The site should be simple and easy to navigate. Don't hide stuff. I hate going to sites looking for a particular thing and can't find it. Sometimes a search window can be valuable. Obviously you need really good images and videos. Videos tell a much better story than still pictures. You can take videos with your smartphone and upload them to YouTube in minutes. Then they can be embedded into your website easily.

Make the Contact information easy to find. It's most often under a button labeled "Contact Us". And, don't just put an email address. Put the phone number, the hours that you're open and any other means of contact that you have. People get aggravated if they need you quickly and they email you and you don't answer for two days. By the way, I no longer pay for any yellow page advertising. All that money goes into website development and maintenance. Only old people use the yellow pages..... (Pardon that remark. It was for my golfing buddies..... all over 65 and none of them have smartphones)

I tried to buy a car online recently and emailed two dealers. No answer in two days, so I went to a third dealership and bought a car that day. When the first two did return my emails on the third day, I informed them what car I bought and where. I told them why and never received a reply.

It's also a good idea to put in a permanent "email us " pop up. It should be in the same place on every page of your site. People like that and are more likely to contact you. Also, It's almost a necessity to include your company's Facebook page on your website. People should be able to "Like" your page from your website. They should also be able to see your latest Facebook posts.

Content

There are a lot of websites out there that have different ideas of what content they should have. The concept of showing all of your products and services goes without saying, but what makes you different from anyone else? A relatively new concept is CMS. Content management systems. This is a type of website that is composed of multiple blogs. You have buttons down the side and each has a different category. In my jewelry site we have categories such as how to choose your diamond, how to propose, celebrity gemstone stories, interesting jewelry facts, a wedding planner guide, ancient gemstone lore and more. Each of these categories are blogs. The term blog comes from the term web log. A better way to look at it would be a series of magazine type articles on a particular subject. CMS websites allow you to build any number of blogs. The positive feedback I get from our site tells me that many of today's younger shoppers appreciate and are impressed with all sorts of information on a product they want to buy. What is valuable more and more today is interaction with your customers. More and more young people want to communicate with you. They want your opinions and they want to give you theirs. They are certainly more impressed with our website than many others that have that picture of the sales staff. More about my website later in this chapter.

E-Commerce

A question is whether or not to have items for sale on your website. I see no downside. Best case is someone will come to your site, see an item and buy it. In my site, I have several dozen estate pieces for sale on the site. I find most customers see it online, but come to the store to see it before they buy. It's not easy to compete with the global big guys, but the purpose of small brick and mortar store website is to inform local potential customers. Not many people will travel a thousand miles to shop for a pair of shoes.

SEO - Search Engine Optimization

This is an annoying but often a necessary expense. If you build a website, even correctly, a competitor can pay an SEO company a monthly fee to keep them at the top of the search engines. Sometimes it's a major advantage to come up first. If the first on a page get the hit most of the time, their likely to get more customers..... assuming their brand attracts the person clicking on them. It depends on your business and your website, whether it will pay you to make that investment.

How to Make Your Website

OK, I've given you a lot of good advice but, like a lot of advice I've given you so far, this could be expensive. The first question is how important is it for you to have a real good website. If it's crucial to your business, and by now you should know that answer, you will have to "Git er Done!" There will be several ways to design and build a website. One way is to learn how to do it yourself. I did that with the use of a Dummy's book. But, I'm semi retired (I work 50 hours per week minus two hours per day to play nine holes) and had the time to learn how to do it, time to research how to design it, time to build it and now time to maintain it. I also have the advantage of a techie background. So I'm a rare jewelry store owner.

Your options are to have a friend or relative do it; have a cheap company do it; or an expensive company can do it. The friend or relative is usually a huge mistake. You can't criticize them or fire them easily. Whoever you hire, you must have control. You want to have it done your way. Many companies have a template. All their websites look the same. They just change your pictures. You might find a competitor's site you like. Ask your potential company if they can make your site like that one. If all you want is a picture of your sales staff, go online and use a free template and you'll have a site in ten minutes.

Getting a really great website designed and constructed is a royal pain, but in the new business world, websites and social media are the new marketing. It's a ton of work, but you have to compete with the big box stores and the Internet. We have to be crazy to go into retail, so we have to pay the price. One of your first new hires as your business grows will have to be the VP of Marketing. (You can call the position a VP, but you need a managerial level person). I would be reluctant to hire a college graduate who majored in marketing, because they are trained to work for big companies. You need to hire someone that will learn to market your micro level business ..... on the job. Make them read this book.

Addendum

As a business consultant, one of my priorities is to stay ahead of the pack....to use what I've learned in business to keep up and go beyond conventional thinking. In 1976. I started a part-time jewelry business in an office with a $700 investment. That developed into a full time profitable operation in the 1980's. In the early 1990's my business reached a plateau. It was going nowhere. I was working 60 hours per week and making very little money. My business was somewhat profitable so I owed taxes but had no cash. I hired E-Myth Consultant Tom Bardeen to help me learn to develop and grow my business. With his coaching we grew the company to a $1,000,000. operation with 10 employees. I enjoyed learning how to REALLY run a business after "running" a business for years, so I conveniently retired from John P. Kuehn Fine Jewelers and formed my own consulting company. My number one client is Kuehn Sisters Diamonds. My daughters are now in charge of day to day operations and I am their business/marketing consultant. In so doing I have researched social networking and website design and taken it step above what you usually see.

The new site, http://www.kuehnsisters.com not only incorporates their slogan and USP, but we included a whole lot of other stuff. On the left side is our Facebook Page integrated into the website. It shows all the posts as they happen and it shows thumbnail pictures of 30 or 40 of our latest of almost 4000 "Likes". Then there are a series of blogs. There are articles on "How to Choose your Diamond, Wedding planning, the Ancient Lore of Diamonds, suggestions on how to propose, Celebrity Diamonds and the stories that go with them and several more categories. These are all separate blogs that are integrated into the front page of the website. It will be the responsibility of the marketing manager to come up with one or two new articles per week. As new articles are posted, they are announced in Facebook so all of the Facebook fans can go to the website to see the article if they want to.

There are two other categories that are important. One is the Kuehn Sisters Video Showcase. This is a unique way to sell items in the store online. It involves a one or two minute video of the girls showing an item for sale. They discuss it and try it on and show close-ups. Basically each item shows up as an article: Sapphire and diamond earrings for example. In the article is a still picture of the item, along with a complete description and a price. There is a button to press to see the video of the item, which is stored on YouTube. We also have a separate connected and linked website just for our antique and estate jewelry. On this site I have added E-Commerce, so the public can actually buy items from the site. Using a separate website makes us still easier to find through internet search engines. By the way, what we have found, however, is most buyers are local and they come in the store and see the item before they buy it.

So, there it is. The idea is to create traffic of all kinds.... traffic that will buy from the website and/or buy from the store. Also, we have been examining the statistics, but it looks like no one under 40 will check out the brick and mortar store without first checking out the website. So the goal is to continually change and update the site to make it convince people to actually go to the store. We're not sure how popular this experiment is going to be, but we'll watch and see. The one sure thing is the technology is changing so fast along with social media marketing that three years from now the design and marketing thrust will be nothing like it is today.

Chapter 13

Social Networking

Note: Everything you read in this chapter is outdated.... Social networking is changing on a day-to-day basis. Facebook may cease to exist by the time you read this. It will be up to you, the entrepreneur to gather and study all of the latest social networking activities, and to use and take advantage of the changes and evolutions.

If your newspaper advertising rep came to you and said "I have a deal".... You can supply a nice picture and write a two or three sentence message like:

"Check out our new line of ladies shoes by Pierre O'Hara. We have many to choose from and prices start at $35.00. See more pictures at our website http://www.oursite.com"

Now, let's say he told you he would guarantee to get this ad to 2000 people who already know and like your store....and your cost.... absolutely free. Are you going to do it??????

Facebook

I know this hurts...just sit down and bear it! Also, I don't want to hear the horror stories of bad experiences with online predators of various types... There are more live predators than online ones and there are ways to deal with it. I'll use the example of the E-Harmony type sites. Stories are broadcasted and rebroadcasted about how someone hooked up with a predator thinking it was her soul mate. Some horror stories are true, I'm sure, but I'll bet that a hundred times more predators are picked up in bars.....

According to comScore's 2010 U.S. Digital Year in Review, the site's unique and daily visitors rose by 38 and 69 percent, respectively. Page views rocketed 71 percent, and overall time spent on the site increased 79 percent, making it the Web's leading site in that category. In fact, in February, 2011 it surpassed Google as the most visited site.

It was launched in 2004 from a Harvard dorm room and subsequently credited with applying the word "friend" as a verb. As of 2014 Facebook boasts 1,310,000,000 users. 640,000,000 minutes per month are being spent on Facebook. And there are 54,200,000 Pages

While the site explains that Facebook is a social utility helping people communicate more effectively with their friends, family and coworkers, the public—namely, business owners—have found a way to harness the power of the site for marketing purposes. A growing number of businesses are using Facebook to find new customers, keep current customers informed and interested, and access demographic information.

What is it about?

The usual post consists of a picture and a short statement... sometimes there's a link to some website. O.K., many if not most of Facebook posts are lame..... My personal Facebook friends are mostly younger relatives.... 20 – 35. They post things like "Oh darn, I have to shovel snow off my car", " I just got a box of candy from my secret admirer", "I hate going out in this weather it's too windy", Here's a picture from the restaurant I'm eating at", etc., etc. There are also a slew of higher level posts... I have a business consultant who I friended, who comes out with a quote of the day. He said today "When you get along with people, they are far more likely to "get along" with your ideas".

I have 100+ personal friends and several dozen pages (business Pages) I "like". These are business friends and business competitors. Sometimes you can learn from your competitors. I "thumb" through the various posts twice a day, to see what's going on. I rarely make any posts myself. I find that my young audience rarely understands my humor. I often make comments on other's posts.... and they rarely understand the humor. (I know.... My humor needs work) My main reason for existing on Facebook is that you need a personal profile in order to construct business "pages". Also, there are millions of people who spout politics ad absurdum. I don't friend anyone from either party. I try to keep politics outside of business as much as possible.

By the way, I'm not going to waste my time or yours giving you instructions on how to start your Facebook adventure. I recommend the Dummy's Book of Facebook Marketing. Read the whole thing and then go step by step with it and you'll be as advanced as you need to be.

Important Note:
I've noticed many marketing gurus suggest you have one of your younger employees handle and maintain Facebook. Ask yourself this: "Would I hire this person as my Marketing Director?" Are you going to trust your marketing to some young kid who probably posts how he/she is going to get out of working today......? Has that kid read and understood the marketing chapters in this book? If you have a Marketing Director and he/she understands, by all means give him the job. Have Him read the Dummies Book if necessary. If not, YOU are the marketing director. READ THE BOOK!!!

O.K. You have your business page set up, so now it's time to develop a following. Ask all your friends to "like" your business Page, but that's just a weak starting point. You want quality fans not quantity. Put Facebook signs up in your business, on your website. Inform customers that you'll have special announcements and deals only through Facebook. The idea of Facebook is to communicate, not to sell. I find about three posts per week is about right. I try to provide interesting information and always point them to the website. The overall value of Social Media is to increase business. Your website is designed to sell directly to the public or to get the public to visit your business. We announce events in the store. We announce contests and then we announce the winners, with pictures of how happy they were. In my daughters' store we try to post pictures of the newly engaged couple with their new ring. We consistently gain one to two new "fans" per day, seven days per week. It's a good idea to be relevant, polite and not pushy. It takes time to develop the following, but in the longer run, when you have several thousand friends, one announcement can bring in many customers. The only downside is that Facebook could be gone a year from now and new media concepts can take over. You just have to be ready for change and be able to adapt. In fact, lately Facebook is trying to increase their income. They don't allow all of your friends to see all of your posts. In fact, they choose the posts they feel you should see. (Yes, that bothers and insults me). The only way a business can speak to all their friends is now to pay for the post to be upgraded. However, it's not very expensive yet.

Advertising on Facebook

Another way to find new friends is to actually spend a meager amount of money with Facebook ads..... Again, if you decide to do this, get the Dummies Book. The unique thing about Facebook ads is you can advertise exclusively to a very well defined demographic group of people. This information they get from your profile is used to define the group, or narrow it down to a very sharp target. For example, they can send the ad only to single females between 25 and 30 who make more than $50,000, who reside within 20 miles of your location. Try that with your newspaper or TV station.

The goal is to increase the number and quality of your likes. And, once they "like" you, you can communicate with them on a regular basis.

I just got an email from my Cable TV rep and he attached an article that showed you don't increase sales through Social Media connections. I'm not sure how the study was set up, but the simple logic that several thousand people are aware of things you say and do in your business can't be a negative process. These are people who "liked" you. They want to know what you are saying. Maybe they won't buy the product you posted today, but when they need such a product, there's a good chance they will buy it from you. I asked my cable rep which of his TV stations Millennials were watching and I got a snicker. He then sent me an article that Millennials watch TV on their laptops. And, coincidentally he sells commercials on the shows they watch through the cable company's Wifi.

Facebook Vs. Your Website

I've noticed numerous businesses have not invested in websites, but many of them have Facebook pages. That's like putting up a billboard ad that doesn't include your address. And, until recently, the two entities were separate and distinctly different. At best, Facebook included the link to the website and the website had the Facebook link. But, now the cutting edges have gone forward and new technology has allowed us to integrate the two together. The concept is called RSS feeds. Websites, now have the ability to show as part of the home page, your Facebook posts, live, as well as thumbnail pictures of the most recent fans. I discussed in detail what the new approach to website design is looking like in the last Chapter. The fact remains that a substantial number of your new customers will not physically approach your business until they first check out the website. If your website is lame or non-existent, they might associate that with what to expect if they visited the business. Historically, this has been the 20 to 30 year olds, however, there are a ton of old people now entering the social networking world.

Twitter and the Others

Twitter is a little different than Facebook in that you're only allowed to post 140 characters or spaces. This usually includes a short statement that refers to a link which is included in the tweet. There are still many lame posts, but I believe the main objective of a Twitterer is to follow people they want to hear from. What did Lady Ga Ga say yesterday. What does Justin Bieber have to say today... and you read their lame posts. However, there's another facet to this medium....There are many Twitterers who post meaningful, interesting and informative stuff.... I shouldn't mention politicians at this point, but most of them regularly tweet. Many businesses tweet to their followers, just as they post on Facebook to their "likes". Twitter started out as more of a business to business site than a business to consumer site. It's also not as localized as Facebook. In Facebook most of your friends are local, where Twitterers have no such boundaries. I have previously recommended Facebook as an area of concentration for retailers and localized businesses and Twitter for online business to business companies, however, Twitter is gaining on Facebook for consumer to consumer "conversations". But, it can't hurt a local company to do both... If you've mastered Facebook, at least get a personal Twitter account and see what you think.

Following is a blog post by Beth Hrusch. Beth is Senior Editor at Interact Media, a website content development service.
www.flickr.com/photos/7son75/2573812829/

Companies both large and small are jumping on the social media bandwagon. Some have large marketing budgets, and some—not so much. One of the great things about social media for marketing is that it gives everyone an equal chance to reach their target markets, regardless of the money they have to spend. Twitter, for example, is becoming recognized as a pretty agile tool for businesses of all sizes.

When you use Twitter, you're tapping into a resource that can help you engage your audience, increase brand awareness and generate new leads. If you're new to it, here are a few tips for using Twitter to promote your business:

1. Find your groups- Once you start your business account, link up with like-minded users with twittgroups, a tool that helps you

find the people who share your interests, and therefore may be interested in your company. A neat feature of this tool is the fact that you can use it to join groups from other social sites such as Facebook and LinkedIn. You can also create a group here— a great way to draw others to you.

2. Start conversations. Once you gather together your groups, start engaging with them. This is called "tweeting". You can share industry news, links, photos and videos, etc. Of course, you only have 140 characters on Twitter, including links, so just include what's absolutely necessary and shorten your links with bit.ly or another URL shortener.

3. Follow and be followed. Twitter allows you to follow anyone you find interesting, and they can follow you back. "Following" is really just a way for people to stay in touch on Twitter, by receiving updates, latest posts, etc. from each other in real time. You can protect your profile, which would require others who want to follow you to request it. Otherwise, anyone can follow you, and you can remove them later if you wish. For businesses, this is the way to communicate

with groups and know that those people are receiving the latest tweets.

4. Post live updates. Twitter is a handy way to update your followers in real time. Since it is so compatible with mobile devices (remember the 140 character limit), you can send people comments and news from wherever you are. Are you attending a trade show or conference? Use Twitter to tell everyone what's going on, on the spot. Even the CEO who's too busy to keep up with the company blog can fire off a tweet from the road and stay in touch.

5. Make announcements. Are you a retailer who's having a sale? Launching a new product or service? Hiring a new executive? Post a note or link to a press release through a Twitter tweet. You can even alert followers when you have a special coming up, or want to entice them with a sneak preview.

6. Promote. Business promotion accounts for about 75% of all marketing activity on social media. Post links to your latest blogs, white papers, articles and videos, so others can easily access them. Start discussions about topics related to your industry. Invite feedback. This establishes your authority,

which is ultimately the best way to promote your business.

Twitter can be an effective marketing tool if used properly. Even if you've never used social media for marketing before, it's easy to get started with it and become part of a community of potential customers, and even fellow industry thought leaders. Update your account regularly, and take time to build the relationships that lead to sales. Your efforts will pay off in increased exposure and connections that expand your customer base.

From Discussions with the "Experts"

As of the second half of 2014, Facebook is declining and Twitter is leveling off. Young people are looking elsewhere because their parents are monitoring them on Facebook and Twitter. Parents and grandparents are communicating with their children and grandchildren… they are texting each other routinely. Now you must get the dummy's book on two up-and-coming sites…. Pinterest and Instagram. I know it's aggravating to get the hang of one site only to find out its outdated and new sites are taking over. I am presently talking to a new company about managing our social networking and website marketing and working with us on content. It will be worth a monthly fee to have some professional management in this important area of marketing.

Finally, who knows what will be five years from now???? Facebook started in 2004 but it didn't become viral until several years later. I believe marketing principles have remained the same, but technology is changing the delivery. As businesses, we have to keep our heads out of the sand....observe what's going on and take advantage of new technology as soon as it becomes viable. I remember phones you had to dial.... If we needed to make a phone call when we were in a car, we had to travel for hours sometimes until we found a roadside phone booth. Remember the first cell phone was a small satchel you put on the floor of your car. That wasn't too long ago. What will we be carrying in our pockets ten years from now? I doubt it will even make phone calls.

Chapter 14

Organizational Charts

You would think that Org Charts are only for big business, and they usually are. However, they are a very important tool in the business development process. An Org Chart shows all of the positions in the organization. It shows the major categories and it shows who reports to whom. It shows all of the positions and who is filling those positions. If someone is promoted or leaves, you can see what position becomes available. If one person is occupying multiple positions, you can see what position can be filled to take up some of the slack. In the beginning of a business, the owner takes almost all the positions. As the business grows, people are hired to take his place. Eventually all positions will be filled by different people.

The major categories are similar between big business and small retailers, but areas of emphasis are obviously different. The major areas for a small retailer are:

1. Administration and Planning – The CEO – He or she runs the show. As the company grows, this job gets more into planning and goal setting and less into day-to-day operations. In the beginning,

the owner fills this job... along with many others. But as growth takes place, it comes to a point where the owner can recruit and hire a CEO. Yes, that can and does happen.

2. Finance – includes bookkeeping, accounting, inventory management, financial reporting and research
3. HR – All employee related processes and requirements
4. Marketing – includes Information technology and web design and marketing research and planning, social networking
5. Operations – Basically the store manager and under that position is the sales manager and staff, the service manager (or the production manager if you make products) and staff and the facilities manager (building and grounds maintenance, remodeling) and staff

A generic chart that can be used in many small businesses.

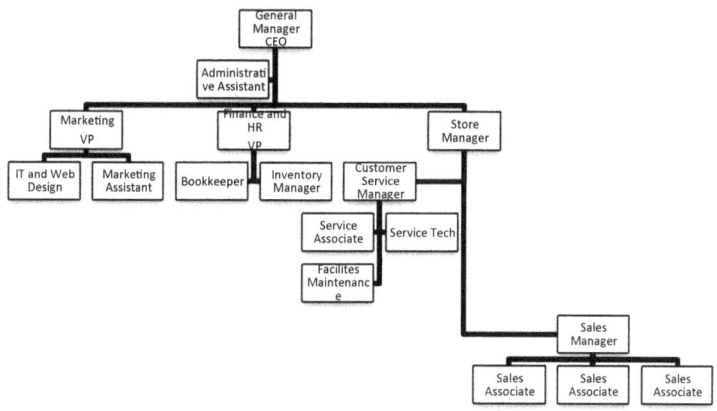

There is another box that all org charts must have and that is the ownership of the company. Sometimes it's shown on the chart and sometimes it's implied. Usually it consists of the Board of Directors. In small companies, it might be just one person. In large corporations the board consists of big stockholders that also represent the small stockholders. It's their job to hire the company CEO and provide short and long term plans, objectives and guidelines for the growth of the company.

If you are a small family owned business, you might have problems deciding on how to pay each family member. In too many cases there is a partnership. In my experience, partnerships increase the likelihood of the business failing by two or three thousand percent. Anyway, to determine compensation, see which box or boxes in the Org Chart each partner is occupying. The pay they get is that amount you would pay an employee to perform that job. Then, at the end of the year, if you are equal partners you split the net profits that you do not reinvest in the business. This also works for husband and wife (or equivalent) teams.

Chapter 15

Job Descriptions

In my early days in the jewelry business, I used to hire someone and on the first day, hand he or she over to the sales staff and commanded "Make her feel at home and show her what she has to do". That's how I took care of the new employee training process. When the business was very small, this was not a major issue, but productivity and the value of employees increases greatly when the employee knows exactly what's expected of them.

Having a formal job description tells the employee clearly what they are expected to accomplish. It helps for recruiting, it helps you set goals and it helps you measure job performance. It's also good for settling any disputes that come up.

I remember an incident that occurred before I learned about business development: My wife and I noticed there were three sales employees on the sales floor when a customer blew her nose and placed the used Kleenex on the counter. The used Kleenex was on the counter all day. They'd show an item to a customer and move out of the way of the Kleenex. I explained to my wife that since we were only paying two dollars more than minimum wage, we can't expect an employee to get rid of the Kleenex on their own. Until they are higher paid and be expected to think for themselves, they would have to be asked to pick up the Kleenex. My wife, from the office, finally signaled one of the sales girls to pick it up and she mouthed back the words "it's not in my job description". How many times have we heard that one. My wife finally came out of the office with a paper towel and solved the problem. When we started instituting job descriptions, it was very interesting to note that all sales employees should check and clean the cases every hour on the hour. We happily agreed to the suggestion. And that brings up another facet of the disclaimer placed at the end of each agreement. The last sentence: *"The Company may change this Position Agreement, and the employees' responsibilities, at any time."* I've never had to use it, but I have had employees that were sticklers for the rules. They were afraid they were being forced to do something others weren't or they were not getting privileges others were getting.

The Components of a Job Description

1. Job Title
2. Pay Grade or Range
3. What Position does this position report to
4. What positions, if any, report to this position
5. Daily hours of operation
6. Summary and Objectives of the job
7. The necessary qualifications for this job
8. Job Duties and Responsibilities

The Three Month and One Year Re-evaluation

A very important and valuable way to improve employee performance is to re-evaluate, review and revise the job description. It can be very valuable to announce when you hire someone that in three months you are going to meet with that person and go over that job description. There might be things that need to be added or removed. The key thing is that you, the supervisor, work with the employee to revise the job description. The employee will have input as to increasing or decreasing the number and kinds of activities. You the supervisor can discuss adding some responsibilities and raising the wage or remove certain activities that get in the way. The employee will be much more productive when contributing to his or her own job description.

If you institute this program with existing employees, I would advise your making up each job description for each employee. Then you can meet with each employee to get their input. Then enter the revised description into the operations manual and mark it for review in three months. After that it might help to do this every year. Employees might show you ways to increase their productivity each year in an effort to increase their wages. This is a much more productive way to give annual salary increases just for being in the job for a year.

From Monster.com is the following job description of a retail salesperson:

Description: Retail Salesperson

Retail Salesperson Job Purpose: Serves customers by helping them select products.
Retail Salesperson Job Duties:

- Welcomes customers by greeting them; offering them assistance.

- Directs customers by escorting them to racks and counters; suggesting items.

- Advises customers by providing information on products.

- Helps customer make selections by building customer confidence; offering suggestions and opinions.

- Documents sale by creating or updating customer profile records.

- Processes payments by totaling purchases; processing checks, cash, and store or other credit cards.

- Keeps clientele informed by notifying them of preferred customer sales and future merchandise of potential interest.

- Contributes to team effort by accomplishing related results as needed.

Skills/Qualifications: Listening, Customer Service, Meeting Sales Goals, Selling to Customer Needs, Product Knowledge, People Skills, Energy Level,

Dependability, General Math Skills, Verbal Communication, Job Knowledge

I included this job description from www.entrepreneur.com because not only does it give a good example of a job description, but it shows what it would take to hire your replacement

General Manager Job Description

Key job tasks of general manager

1. Planning administration

- Provide leadership and vision to the organization by assisting the Board and staff with the development of long range and annual plans, and with the evaluation and reporting of progress on plans.
- Oversee preparation of an Annual Report summarizing progress on short and long range plans.
- Research and write discussion papers, analysis documents and proposals as needed to assist the organization in determining and meeting its long and short term goals.

2. HR management

- Recruitment and contracting of company and project staff;
- Employee development, and training;
- Policy development and documentation;

- Employee relations;
- Performance management and improvement systems;
- Employment and compliance to regulatory concerns and reporting;
- Company-wide committee facilitation including planning, production, staff and
- Board of Directors, including arranging meetings and agendas, attending and minuting meetings;

3. Project management:

- Manage hire and distribution of music scores and parts, including any performing rights payments.
- Oversee the booking of tours this includes: venue liaison from negotiating the deal to distribution of audience questionnaires, programs and merchandise.
- Oversee organization of company transport, subsistence and accommodation.
- Liaise with Production Manager to oversee hire and delivery / transport of all technical and production equipment.

4. Marketing and PR:

- Manage advertising opportunities in other theatre program, press and at venues.
- Organize the availability of company members for media/PR events as necessary.

- Oversee content, production and distribution of all marketing and publicity materials (posters, program, flyers, mail outs, brochures etc) with director, designer and project manager.
- Manage press development;
- Co-ordinate the invitation of potential future promoters and supporters of the company.

5. Financial management

- Provide recommendations regarding investments and cash strategies.
- Oversee preparation of annual budget, regular variance statements and annual audit.
- Provide vision regarding overall financial health of the company.
- Provide vision and leader ship in long - range fiscal planning to ensure the continuity and solvency of the company.
- Provide recommendations regarding effective utilization of long and short term debt, including refinancing and purchasing/sales.
- Oversee fundraising efforts.

7. Production/QC:

- Insure accurate documentation of production and quality control data and records.
- Direct and oversee site production activities and personnel.

- Oversee and ensure high safety standards at all times.
- Direct production activities to insure safety and compliance with quality control standards, regulatory compliance, and lease agreements.
- Oversee and/or ensure good housekeeping at site at all times.

6. Administrative management

- Ensure client and vendor file integrity (documents, analytical information where required, communication notations, etc.).
- Maintain general oversight and insure accuracy of records including A/R, A/P, Inventory, etc.
- Assist in development of forms and tools to increase company efficiency and risk management.

III / Job specification of general manager job description

1. A minimum of five years of experience in business management, planning and financial oversight.
2. A minimum of five years of experience in personnel management, including hiring, supervision, evaluation and benefits administration.
3. A minimum of three years of experience working with a board of directors and committees.

4.   College graduate or equivalent experience.
5.   Proven skills in business and financial management.
6.   Demonstrated ability to work with student member - owners.
7.   Demonstrated ability to work in a proactively diverse and inclusive organization.
8.   Excellent, proven interpersonal, verbal and written communications skills.
9.   Demonstrated ability to manage and supervise a staff team.
10. Effective problem - solving and mediation skills.
11. Demonstrated ability to share skills and knowledge with others.
12. Proficiency with office computer equipment and software.
13. Demonstrated ability to multi - task and work in a fast - paced office setting.
14. Proven ability to cope with conflict, stress and crisis situations.

III / Compensation and benefits
1.   Not as much as you would make if you had a real job.

Following is a job description I used in the jewelry store. It's kind of involved, but if you want to see the type of detail you can get to cover as many bases as possible, this is an example:

Job Description
Sales Associate

Results Statement: This position is accountable for retaining clients by providing product knowledge, services and information they will perceive as emotionally satisfying, and by creating and implementing systems to allow others to do the same.

Reporting Positions: There are no other positions reporting directly to this position at this time.

Technical Work:

Daily Activities and responsibilities:
a) Putting jewelry into showcases.
b) Keeping jewelry & displays wiped and fingerprint free. Make sure that everything is ticketed properly, clean and attractively displayed. (see Sales Associate Responsibility Check Sheet)

c) Maintaining the appearance of the sales floor and displays. Keep showcases, windows, back room and stock clean and orderly.
d) Selling merchandise (knowing the salability of the merchandise)

e) Developing a complete knowledge of the merchandise. Learning features, and benefits through catalogs, trade magazines, and independent study.

f) Putting new inventory into stock (once entered by customer service)

g) Decorating showcases and designing of front window displays.

h) Putting jewelry in safes

1. Customer Relations
   - Basic Telemagic – Our Point of sale computer system
   - Greet each and every customer with a smile (if you're already with a customer, at least acknowledge that you have seen the customer come in and let them know someone will be with them shortly.)
   - The gathering of customer information for our wish list
   - Learning the customer to insure quality service (getting to know the customer helps you sell them the jewelry they want). Listening to the customer is very important.
   - Answer the phone with the store's phone script. " Hello, this is Jeanie at John P. Kuehn Fine Jewelers, when it has to be unique, how may I help you?"
   - Inspecting and cleaning customer's jewelry

- Maintain a good, neat, professional appearance in accordance with dress code.
- Providing minor repairs when necessary (watch batteries and shortenings)
- Performing other duties as assigned.

General Standards

General Standards for all employees:

1. The primary concern is for the Client. Client needs will be met in a manner consistent with the company Mission.
2. Every employee will present themselves with the highest level of honesty, competency and professionalism at all times. Acts of dishonestly will result in disciplinary action or dismissal.
3. All clients and fellow employees will be greeted and treated in a friendly, professional manner. Remember, we are in the Relationship Business – Not just the Service Business!
4. Clients will be treated with respect at all times. Use of phrases like "Yes Sir", "No Mam", "Please" and "Thank You" are required during conversations with clients. Avoid slang or lazy sounding language.

5. The Telephone will be answered in a friendly and courteous manner. Phone calls should be answered by the third ring.
6. All telephone calls will be returned as promptly as possible, with a goal of returning all calls within two hours and never later than the next business day.
7. Personal calls are to be held to a minimum. Long or extended personal calls are not permitted.
8. Effort will be made to help employees / peers perform to the best of their ability and to meet company and department standards.
9. All work will be performed according to the developing Operations Manual, as well as in the spirit of the company's objectives.
10. All employees will make understanding the Client's needs a Priority.
11. All work will be neat and accurate. All correspondence will be presented in a neat and professional manner.
12. Desks, work areas and company vehicles and equipment will be kept neat and clean at all times. Always seek to sustain a professional appearance.
13. All documents, records and files will be maintained inside filing cabinets and shelving units in an organized, orderly and accessible manner.
14. All invoices and receipts must be given to the Bookkeeper promptly after products/services have been acquired and the employee has returned to the office. Either turn them in with your daily

paperwork (for technicians) or put them in the Bookkeeper's mailbox.

15. The security and confidentiality of files and all business matters will be upheld at all times. Breach of confidentiality will result in loss of position. All proprietary company information will be held as strictly confidential.

16. No conversations regarding compensation will be discussed with anyone other than your immediate supervisor or the General Manager.

17. Socializing will not impede work flow. All employees will respect each other's time and need for concentration.

18. All employees will strive to independently initiate follow-through and take action in order to produce effective results without supervision.

19. All employees will use good judgment in making decisions and understand the value of saying "I don't know the answer...but I will find out"

20. All employees will ask questions when in doubt.

21. All employees will utilize established channels of communication whenever possible to minimize interruptions. These include the company mailboxes, daily reports and weekly meetings. However, employees should never fail to seek advice or guidance when immediate help is needed.

22. All employees will prioritize, plan and utilize time in a manner to be most effective.

23. All ideas for improvement will be submitted to immediate supervisor during weekly meetings. Employees are encouraged to submit ideas in the form of an Action Plan.
24. All employees will strive to create simplicity in our business by documenting systems and writing Action Plans.
25. Employees will enjoy learning, creating, and improving systems.
26. All Action Plans will be evaluated and revised as needed prior to implementation.
27. Action Plans for all technical work will be developed and maintained in the company Operations Manual.
28. A written letter of resignation is necessary when resigning / leaving the company. Such written notice will be presented to immediate supervisor and the General Manager.
29. Employees will be pro-active, anticipate problems, and demonstrate enthusiasm about their work. Employees will strive to have fun and to be fun to work with.
30. Employees will not use propane or offensive language, nor make disparaging remarks about clients, co-workers or supervisors.
31. All employees will work together to clean shelves, dishes, showcases and to set up at opening and take down at closing

This job description is not intended to be a "legal" contract. It does not alter the employee's at-will employment status. This job description is simply a document designed to encourage a more agreeable working relationship and a greater understanding between each employee and his/her manager. It is intended to describe, where possible, the mutual expectations and accountabilities of both the employee and the supervisor. The Company may change this job description, and the employees' responsibilities, at any time

Note: It is extremely important that when and if you construct your own set of employee job descriptions, that you have an attorney check them for legality and potential problems. The intent is for the job description to be an agreement between employee and manager rather than a contract. It should not be a legally binding contract. You might need a lawyer to tell you how to change the description, so it's not a legal contract and so the employee understands that. I'm sure the laws differ in each state.

Chapter 16

Action Plans

What is an Action Plan

An Action Plan covers the detailed steps you must go through to achieve a goal or solve a problem. The plan includes the estimated time, the people responsible, needed resources and potential barriers.

When a manager needs his people to accomplish a goal, he or she can write a detailed action plan which shows everyone what they are expected to do and when. Providing a written plan is a much more productive way to accomplish a goal than merely telling your employees they need to accomplish a particular goal and let them figure it out.

However, the most practical and productive way to use action plans is when an employee comes to a manager with a problem. In many cases an employee knows what the problem is and would like to have it solved. So, I will discuss in the next chapter how to convince employees that they will have a better working situation if they provide the solution to their problems rather than the supervisor. This procedure adds to the company's business development plan, it saves a huge amount of time for the manager and when a plan adds to the smooth running of a company it's entered into the operations manual and becomes a permanent asset of the company.

The following may be used as a template and sent to each member of the company so they can save it on their computer's desktop. When they need it, finding it will not be a problem.

Your Company's Action Plan Template

1. The Objective of this Action Plan is to:

2. The plan author is:

3. Step-by-step details:

4. Resources Needed

5. Potential Barriers or problems with the plan

6. The person(s) performing the step-by-step are:

7. Estimated completion date:

8. O.K.'d by _____

Chapter 17

Time Management and One-On-One Employee Meetings

A Research Project: How You Spend Your Time

According to an Intuit Business Blog (How Small Businesses get started and Keep running – Infographic in the Trends section), business owners spend 14 hours per week conducting business services, six hours on sales, five hours on communication, three hours on financial management, three hours on web management, 2 hours on getting paid (I guess it takes a while to count it), two hours on contact management, two hours on employee management and two hours on other.

Now this study was obviously done for "small businesses" which are quite a bit larger than the businesses we're talking about. I would guess 50 or more employees. We need to figure out how us real small business owners spend our time. I know it will be a valuable exercise for you to make a chart of all your working hours in a week. You can make an Excel spreadsheet with day of the week across the top (Of course include Saturday and Sunday) and

6:00, 6:30, 7:00, etc. down the left side. Fill in this chart and at the end of the week tally it up. I think it will be very informative. It might show you how much time you're wasting, or in what areas do you need to spend more time. To simplify the process, break the sheet into half hour segments and just enter the code for what you did for the majority of that half hour. The codes in the Intuit example don't look practical to me. Try using the following codes:

1. Sales
2. Bookkeeping/finance
3. Social Networking
4. Internet Searching
5. Email Correspondence
6. Customer Service
7. Meetings with employees
8. Marketing
9. Dealing with employees
10. Dealing with Customers
11. Dealing with Salesmen
12. Dealing with Bankers and related
13. Meal

Feel free to add categories and include traveling time to and from one of these categories when assigning the hours. I'll bet you are shocked when you see the summary of your time.

Employee One-On-One Meetings

The Structure

You, as the manager, supervisor, team leader should meet one-on-one with each employee that reports directly to you. You should meet outside the store or office in a neutral, safe, non-threatening environment... Starbucks, Panera Bread for example. Schedule a full half hour so you can adhere to it every week without fail. The location should be free of interruptions. It should be a treat... nice bagels, or donuts, or, if you're inclined a Juice Bar. You pay the bill with petty cash money from the business.

As far as the manager is concerned, the meeting is purely social. Never bring up business. You can discuss sports, movies, TV shows, family stories, etc. It's up to the employee to bring up any troubling business issues. If the employee does bring up any business issues, try to work them out on the spot. If it will take time and research, make sure you follow up in writing within a few days.

The Benefits

This meeting is probably the biggest, most significant time saving activity you can institute. I know, it's a half hour plus transportation, but as you will see later in this Chapter, it will save much more time than it takes. It builds a better relationship between manager and employee. It provides a platform for new ideas. You'll get a better feel for how productive certain employees can be. It will improve accountability and as I mentioned earlier, it will significantly decrease interruptions in the office. Following is a system that alone should pay for this book ten fold.

An Action Plan to Save Your Time And Sanity

If you run a small retail business, you are face to face with employees every minute of every day. Since they see you all the time, they never need to make their own decisions. They simply ask you about everything to your face. As your business is growing, you're hiring more employees and that means more problems and interruptions.

In order to allow you to begin life anew, you need to proclaim a business wide Action Plan. Call it

The Company Communication System

The purpose is to make issue and problem solving simpler, more meaningful and less time consuming. When any employee has an issue or problem that he or she feels the supervisor needs to know about and/or act upon, immediately go to your computer, not the supervisor. Saved on your desktop is a Word file entitled "Company Communication System". Open that file and first place an x in one of the four boxes:

_____   Now or Never, cannot wait!!!

_____   Important, but a solution can wait until our weekly one-on-one meeting

_____ Not greatly important, but you should know about this and an answer would be nice in the next week or so

_____ Not greatly important, but you should know about this. No answer necessary

If you check off number one and you have time, fill in the rest of the form and immediately barge in on the boss. If you don't have time to fill out the form then immediately barge in. If it's number two, fill out the form, print it out and bring it with you to the next employee one-on-one meeting. If it's number three or four, fill it out, copy and paste it into an email and send it to the boss.

The form is simple:

1. The problem is:

2. It affects the following people and activities:

3. I'm doing the following about it:

4. I would like to work on a solution by instituting the following detailed action plan:

* A note to the employee. Number 4 above was not placed in this communications memo as a

punishment; it was placed there for your benefit. If you have a problem in your working environment, you can go to your supervisor and ask he or she to resolve that problem for you. On the other hand, you are the one working in the "trenches". You know what's going on and you will have to abide by whichever action plan solves the problem. Which plan do you want, the supervisor's plan or yours?

Chapter 18

Employee Discipline – Firing

There is no known system of hiring that guarantees you never have to discipline or fire someone. (The Federal Government is the only exception). Your first urge is to ignore a problem. It's hard to discipline someone without causing stress. A manager's goal is to reduce stress to a minimum. Sometimes an employee will cause you too much stress. After awhile he or she can increase everyone's stress. Then, the business is no longer running smoothly. When it gets to that point, you have no choice.

If the problem is sexual harassment, drugs, theft or publically criticizing the Company or it's employees, then there is no choice. No discipline will help. You have to fire the perpetrator. But, short of one of these extremes, you do have some less extreme solutions. The key is to establish an employee discipline system. Everyone should be made aware of this policy. It will obviously go into the operations manual, but every employee should have a copy of your system. If you have to, you can put it into each job description.

The system I'm suggesting has been used in countless big and small businesses, but that doesn't mean you can't change it by adding or subtracting steps. The important issue is you will be following a system. This covers you somewhat from legal encounters. Nothing covers you in full but it helps to follow the same system for all employees and to document in detail every step of the process.

Company Employee Discipline System

Many different possible issues could require the need for some sort of action. Behavioral issues can cause disruptions in the workplace. Performance issues, misconduct or other rules violations can result in the employee not properly performing tasks or meeting goals. Also, the quality of the work might no longer be in acceptable parameters. There are other factors that can cause problems, but common denominator is the manager notices issues that have an unacceptable effect on the company.

Step One: The first reaction can be as simple as a verbal mention of the problem. Casually mention to the employee that you notice there is a problem and you would appreciate an email with an explanation and plans to rectify the situation.

Step Two: If no response to number one, it's time for an email statement that there is a definite problem. Clearly and simply define that problem. Again, ask the employee to respond to the email with an explanation and a plan for rectifying the problem. Make sure you get an email receipt that the employee read the email.

Step Three: Schedule a private meeting. Clearly explain the bad behavior. Explain the consequences and effects. Ask the employee to explain. Ask the employee to write a clear and concise plan to rectify the situation. Warn the employee that this is his/her last chance. Ask if there is anything the manager can do to help. Hand the employee a written version of the complaint. And then, end the meeting on a positive note. You're optimistic the problem will be solved and all will be well.

Step Four: Ask the employee to come to a private office. Have someone else with you. It's better not to be alone. The best time is Monday morning. When you fire someone on Friday afternoon they tend to stew about it all weekend, whereas when you fire someone on Monday morning, they will get into the mode of finding another job sooner. Have a formal copy of all the documentation leading up to this meeting, just in case you need it. Be brief and clear. "I gave you the opportunity to correct the issue on three separate occasions, but your lack of an acceptable response leaves me no choice but to terminate your employment at the Smith Company". At this point, they cannot be surprised. They had to be aware of company policy. Be compassionate but tell them the actual reasons for firing them. Some people tend to sugarcoat. Lay out their options on insurance benefits, unemployment and the final paycheck. Have them leave immediately, but schedule a time they may come back to get their belongings.

Chapter 19

Employee Hiring
The Recruiting Process

Do Not Underestimate The Importance of Hiring

How many times, when we think we need extra help, do you ask your cousin if her daughter is interested in a job? How many times do we hire someone when they walk in the door with a resume? How many times do we hire a relative of another employee? How many times do we put an ad in the paper, get three responses, and hire the blonde?

A company is only as good as its employees. Inexperienced, unmotivated, unambitious, unintelligent employees will not be listed as valued company assets. In fact, they can be its downfall. It might take a little work, but once you find someone, it's just as easy to hire a potential new CEO as an unmotivated drag on the growth of the business. So, why even consider someone who isn't potential CEO material.

I think it was Bill Gates who said his secret to hiring success is he always hired people who were smarter than he. In fact, big corporate CEO's most important activity is hiring. Hiring people smarter than they are makes them successful. The same goes for U.S. Presidents. They are only as good as their trusted advisors. They wouldn't get elected if they didn't hire smart campaign managers.

The Process

1. Plan the complete process in advance

2. Determine Your budget

3. Construct the job description if it's a new position or take it from the operations manual if it's an existing position

4. Decide on which media you will use

5. Design the content of the ads

6. Ask them to submit a resume to Smith Company. It will weed out people who can't figure out where to send the resume. Also, if you are deluged with resumes, you can separate out the applicants that didn't submit the resume with a cover letter. Also, if someone brings in a resume in person, accept it, but after they leave take notes on how well dressed or how presentable they were. I had a young man bring in a resume dressed in jeans whose crotch was just above knee level. I wanted to sit down with him and explain that he was never going to get a job but I was with a customer.

7. Document the process, including the results for entry into the operations manual. From that you will be better equipped to hire that position again.

8. If you have the resources, the new trend in help wanted ads by the big corporations is to have a link published in the help wanted ad, and that link is a professional web page with the story of the company, pictures and a complete description of the job and an application form. They are very professionally done. Search online through the New York Times Classified ads.

Helpful Hints and Suggestions

1. Use the recruiting ad as a way to also advertise the company. "We're growing and successful and we need more employees"

2. Turn your employees into recruiters. Give $100 to the employee who submits a name that turns out to be hired.

3. Consider Social Media for advertising the vacancy.... Facebook, and/or on the website. Use a video asking for the right person.

4. The ad should attract attention. If it's in a long column of ads, it should stand out.

5. Use visuals if possible.

6. Check back with former employees that were successful and left for "better" jobs. They might want to come back.

7. Make your company look friendly.

8. Don't be afraid to hire someone over qualified. We always assume they will drop you and jump to a better job in a heartbeat. If they are that productive, they are worth paying more, and those "better" jobs often are high stress and aggravation.

9. You might suggest to your employees (who are getting a $100 finders fee) that they visit your competitors and seek out their star people.

10. A possible ad could have one or more of your employees explaining how happy they are so you should apply for this job.

11. If you want to hire a great sales associate, advertise for a sales manager trainee. It could very well attract a higher caliber person. Isn't it true that any sales associate you hire is a potential sales manager?

Some Example Ads

1. A picture of Darth Vader saying "Join us or Die" and at the bottom all it said was Smith Marketing

2. "Can You Sell Air?" and at the bottom in small print was a local radio station.

3. WANTED   Young Skinny Wiry Fellows not over Eighteen. Must be expert riders willing to risk death daily. Orphans preferred. Wages $25 per week. Apply Central Overland Express.   (An actual ad for the Pony Express)

4. CUSTOMER SERVICE ASSOCIATE. A 30 year old retail business is looking for highly organized individual to be in charge of all customer service functions, inventory management and related responsibilities. Must have Microsoft Word, and Microsoft Excel experience. Must be able to prioritize multiple tasks and work under deadlines. Must have ability to work as part of a team. Competitive Salary, Excellent Benefits Package. Send resume to: John P. Kuehn Fine Jewelers

5. From a Blog at ABC News: An Executive's longtime secretary had just resigned. She was hard-working, smart, dedicated, funny and thoroughly professional. They had worked together for years, and trusted each other completely. He was so down about her leaving that all he wanted to do was drink a margarita or two and go watch a mindless movie. Instead, he sat down and wrote a classified ad for her replacement. The ad

CAN YOU REPLACE MARY POPPINS?

Our executive secretary has been practically perfect in every way, but now she's moving on. If you can juggle e-mail, voicemail, and notes left on your chair; if you aren't afraid to point out when the boss is being stupid; if you like to make decisions for yourself (and sometimes for other people); and if you keep a magic carpet bag hidden somewhere in your desk, we've got a job for you! ...

In the next few days, the executive was swamped with résumés, faxes, phone calls and e-mail. Almost every letter and call made some mention of Mary Poppins.

Chapter 20

Employee Hiring

The Interview Process

Interviewing

Hopefully you received enough resume's to begin the interview process.   I have found it valuable to hand a job summary sheet to all that hand in a resume. That sheet describes many of the activities of the position as well as the starting wage. This serves to weed out those expecting something different. If they accept an interview after seeing the summary sheet you already know the starting wage is acceptable. When they send their resume via email, you can include the summary sheet when you reply to schedule an interview.

In the early days I had the applicant sit at my desk and I asked a few questions, took a few notes and then gave over the interview to one or two existing employees. I found they had better "intuition" on the matter than I did. Also, they had to work with this person on a day-to-day basis. It was hit and miss process. And, the people we hired were whoever happened to walk in with a resume. I should note that several of those hit and miss people were very successful at their jobs. Once, a girl walked in to the jewelry store looking for a sales job (she had just moved to town with her husband) and as she's telling me about herself, she mentioned she was also an experienced bench goldsmith. I hired her five minutes after she first walked in and she turned out to be the best employee I ever had. I offered her a partnership in the business if she could convince her husband not to move out of town after he got his Master's Degree.

I have, however, gotten burned from time to time but there are more "scientific" ways of choosing the right candidates. Similar techniques are used by the big corporations to hire world-class applicants. The interviewer asks each candidate a series of questions. There are no right or wrong answers, but you grade the answer based on how much you liked the answer. An example would be *"Give me an example of a time you did something wrong. How did you handle it?"* Grade 5 if you liked it a lot down to a 1 for not liking it at all. Hopefully yourself and at least two others will each interview the same applicant. After you're done, you add up the score and compare the scores of each candidate.

It could be as simple as hiring the highest scoring candidate, but some applicants are very convincing when they answer questions. There are people who are gifted interviewees. They sound great, but when they are hired and actually working, it's a different story. Many of these gifted people are in politics.... You really need to spend some additional time with the highest scoring candidates. Take them to lunch or even dinner. Invite them to spend a day at the store and talk to people during a business day. Find ways to learn about them when their guard is down.

Depending on how important this position is, you might want to invest in a background check. Also, you can buy certain tests that given to applicants will reveal how well they might perform at the job. Some test honesty and others describe personality traits.

Following is an article by Joseph Anthony of Microsoft Corporation, from the Microsoft Small Business Resource Center:

Don't ask a job applicant these questions

"You're looking over the résumé of a job candidate. You see that he includes in a list of hobbies his volunteer work with Little League Baseball, and that he went to the same high school as you.

So as part of the getting-to-know-you aspect of the job interview, you ask him if he has any kids and when he graduated.

Great. You've just asked two questions that could leave you open to discrimination lawsuits.

Sometimes clear communication means not collecting background noise that doesn't help you. When you conduct a job interview, you want to ask questions that elicit real information so you can make an informed hiring decision. But you also want to avoid questions that could get you in legal trouble.

"Inappropriate questions during hiring are a major source of lawsuits," says David Curtis, a partner with the Dallas law firm of Gardere Wynne Sewell. "Most illegal questions occur when an employer asks an applicant for information where the answer tends to affect a protected group, such as minorities, women, the disabled, legal aliens and people over 40 years of age, or where the question is not related to essential job functions."

The potential legal problems include, but are not limited to, violations of the Civil Rights Acts of 1964 and 1991, the Age Discrimination in Employment Act of 1967, and the Americans with Disabilities Act of 1991.

Questions must address job requirements

Matthew R. Grabell, an employment attorney with Grabell & Associates in Hackensack, N.J., says that the list of things you cannot ask potential employees about includes:

- Private organizations he or she belongs to
- Religious affiliations
- Date of birth (except when that information is required for satisfying minimum age requirements)
- Lineage, ancestry, national origin, descent, parentage, or nationality
- Names and addresses of relatives other than a spouse and dependent children

- Sex or marital status
- Height or weight, unless you can show that information is justified by business necessity
- Physical or mental disabilities

None of these questions addresses the skills needed to perform a job. "However, it is permissible to ask if the applicant has any disabilities that would prevent him or her from satisfactorily performing the job," Grabell says.

Therese A. Hoehne, director of human resources at Aurora University in Aurora, Ill., gives interviewers at the university a checklist based partly on two publications of the Society for Human Resource Management: "Guidelines On Interview and Employment Application Questions," by Thomas Nail and Dale Scharinger, and "ADA Job Interview Checklist for Supervisors," by Kenneth Pritchard.

"Sometimes you just have a real desire to ask a question like how someone is going to be able to maintain a daily work schedule if she is a young woman responsible for several children. But you can't do that," Hoehne says. "You have to focus on the fact that the person wants to work and whether they say they can do what is necessary."

Grabell says that questions about children, pregnancy and family obligations may make applicants uncomfortable. The questions also may be considered indicative of discrimination if someone is hired and later loses a job after having a child.

Some dos and don'ts

Grabell and other experts give several examples of acceptable and unacceptable questions, including:

OK: What days can you work? What hours can you work?

Not OK: How many children do you have? Do you have a babysitter available if we need you on a weekend?

OK: Do you have any responsibilities that would interfere with traveling for us?

Not OK: Do you have a baby or small child at home?

OK: Are you legally eligible to work in the United States?

Not OK: Are you a U.S. citizen? What country are you from?

OK: This job requires someone who speaks more than one language. What languages do you speak or write fluently?

Not OK: What's your native language?

OK: Have you ever been convicted of a crime?

Not OK: Have you ever been arrested?

OK: You say on your application that you were in the military. What kind of education and experience did you get there?

Not OK: What kind of a discharge did you receive?

OK: Do you have a high school diploma? Do you have a university or college degree?

Not OK: When did you graduate?

Curtis says that even just having a bullet-point list of requirements for the job can help the interviewer stay on track and stay out of trouble.

"The truth is, you don't care about their religious preference or whether they have a car; you care about whether they have the skill set needed to do the job," lawyer Curtis says.

"I think employers sometimes have the misconception that these statutes and rules are somehow tying their hands or impeding their ability to staff their businesses with competent workers who can perform. If they understand these laws, they can see [the rules] are driving them to accomplish what they really want to accomplish anyway."

The following 30 questions came from Career Advice at Monster.com. There are more Questions available there and many more at other sites.

1. Give me an example of a time that you felt you went above and beyond the call of duty at work.
2. Can you describe a time when your work was criticized?
3 Have you ever been on a team where someone was not pulling their own weight? How did you handle it?
4. Tell me about a time when you had to give someone difficult feedback. How did you handle it?
5. What is your greatest failure, and what did you learn from it?
6. What irritates you about other people, and how do you deal with it?
7. If I were your supervisor and asked you to do something that you disagreed with, what would you do?
8. What was the most difficult period in your life, and how did you deal with it?
9. Give me an example of a time you did something wrong. How did you handle it?
10. Have you ever caught any of your co-workers lying and what did you do?
11. Tell me about a time where you had to deal with conflict on the job.
12. If you were at a business lunch and you ordered a rare steak and they brought it to you well done, what would you do?

13. If you found out your company was doing something against the law, like fraud, what would you do?

14. What assignment was too difficult for you, and how did you resolve the issue?

15. What's the most difficult decision you've made in the last two years and how did you come to that decision?

16. Describe how you would handle a situation if you were required to finish multiple tasks by the end of the day, and there was no conceivable way that you could finish them.

17. What are you looking for in terms of career development?

18. How do you want to improve yourself in the next year?

19. What kind of goals would you have in mind if you got this job?

20. If I were to ask your last supervisor to provide you additional training or exposure, what would she suggest?

21. What do you think of your previous boss?

22. Was there a person in your career who really made a difference?

23. What kind of personality do you work best with and why?

24. What are you most proud of?

25. What do you like to do?

26. What are your lifelong dreams?

27. What do you ultimately want to become?

28. What is your personal mission statement?

29. What are three positive things your last boss would say about you?

30. What negative thing would your last boss say about you?

Questions you can ask the candidate's references:

The Best Questions a Reference Checker Can Ask

By: Paul W. Barada, Monster Salary and Negotiation Expert

A simple background check to ensure a candidate didn't lie on his resume or job application isn't enough. It's just the first step. The second, and more important step, is ensuring that the candidate can do what he claims to be able to do. In other words, careful job performance-based reference checking is more important than ever in the employee selection process.

So what are some of the best questions to ask? Once the reference is actually on the phone, the first question to ask is, "How are you acquainted with the candidate?" The answer to this question will accomplish several things. First, it will confirm when, where and whether or not the reference and the candidate have ever worked together, and what the nature of their association was. Did the reference work for the candidate or the other way around, or were they coworkers? Did they work together on a daily basis or just once in a while? The answer to this critical question will allow the reference checker to determine how much weight to give the responses to subsequent questions.

The next question that should be asked is, "How long did you and the candidate work together?" Once again, the length of the association will help establish the credibility of responses to other questions. Obviously, if the reference worked with the candidate for several years, the responses will carry more weight than if the length of their association was only a few months or less.

Next, it's important to ask the reference to describe the candidate's day-to-day responsibilities on the job. This is the point at which the reference checker should be comparing what the candidate's resume says with what the references have to say. The completeness of the answer will also reveal still more about how well the reference really knew the candidate. An evasive or vague answer may suggest, for instance, that the candidate overstated his or her claim to have worked with the reference every day for several months. A red flag should go up if the reference can't describe what the candidate's job responsibilities were with some degree of thoroughness.

Another of the essential questions that must be asked of every reference is, "What do you think the candidate needs to really continue his or her career development and professional growth?" The response to this question can provide invaluable insight into the candidate's suitability for the job to be filled.

Toward the end of the interview, there are other important questions that always should be asked, such as, "Why did the candidate leave?" and "Could the candidate have stayed if he had wanted to?" If the candidate is still working at the same place as the reference, the question becomes, "Why is the candidate contemplating a job change?" Finally, every reference should be asked, "If you were hiring people, would you hire the candidate and, if so, for what type of position?"

While this is not intended to be an exhaustive list of questions reference checkers should ask, it's a starting point that allows you to establish a reference's credibility.

When you have exhausted all of your planned employee selection activities, I would suggest a meeting with your interview committee to discuss each of the top applicants. When you make the decision and inform the final choice, do not make the mistake of informing numbers two and three that they are out of the running. Wait until the final choice reports to work. Then, it still might be advantageous to inform two and three that you expect openings in the near future. If you have a second candidate who you really like, try to create something. It's a waste to just throw out the second and third candidates after the investment in time and money to choose number one.

The next chapter discusses the important process of how to welcome the new employee into your working family.

Chapter 21

Employee Hiring Orientation and Integration

In the past, on the first day of work for a new employee I introduced them to the staff and said "show her what to do". I then went back to more important work... Now, I see research that the first day is the most important day in a particular employees history. First impressions are lasting impressions.

It's also a very grueling experience because a huge amount of information is thrown at the new employee all at once. Trying to grasp everything about the job and the company in one day is an overwhelming amount of stress. Perhaps it would be better to break up the information over several days. The same would be advantageous for the training program. And, if the Operations Manual is up to date on that position, there will be a comprehensive training packet for that position that the employee can take home and study. And, if the operations manual is up to date, they'll have a Company Information packet for all new employees, that tells all about the company.

Another factor that can contribute to the overall performance of the new employee as well as enhancing his or her value to the company is to use the new employee's special knowledge and/or talents. Show them the new job description and ask how they would like to amend or rewrite it to take advantage of their special abilities. That would also enhance the self-confidence and individuality, which characterizes successful employees.

Orientation

Present to the employee a description of the Company. Describe it's history, it's mission, it's organization chart, along with details on how the Company operates... what it sells, what it makes, what it repairs and where and how do all these activities take place.

Depending on the business, it's now time to present a non-compete agreement. You really need a lawyer to write one of these for you because it will be different for every business and in every state. For example, if it's a sales job, can you risk the employee leaving after a year and taking the customer list to his new employer? If you're manufacturing something, do you want to be protected if this employee leaves and starts a new company across the street making the same product?

Then, you need to explain pay, benefits, vacations, sick and absentee policy and disciplinary policy. Fill out all of the legal employment and tax forms. And finally, you explain all the attributes of the job. Present the job description that you wrote and explain you will work with the employee to update, improve and modify as needed. You explain that after the three-month probationary period, you want his or her input as to any additions, subtractions or other changes. Go to the specific working area and introduce fellow workers and the working environment.

Employee Integration

The object of integration is to make the employee feel comfortable, as they become part of the family. If you can make the experience positive as the new employee connects with the new workplace, they will be more productive and stay longer. Of course, every business is different, but it will benefit you and the Company to make the first days and weeks a fun, positive experience. Assigning a mentor, a buddy to take the new employee under his or her wing, so to speak, can be a great help as the new employee is "integrated" into the new environment. Then as the process goes on, it will be time to introduce the new employee to their one-on-one supervisor meetings. Hopefully one of those meetings will be dedicated to the technique of writing action plans.

Chapter 22

Cash Flow

I can't believe I used to run my business every day, but I never knew where I stood financially except for total sales. Once a year my accountant gave me my tax form and I was shocked that I owed taxes. I couldn't figure out how I owed taxes but had no cash. Now, I'm able to glance at my entire financial picture at any time and now I know how much tax I owe at any point in time. And I know exactly why I have no cash.

My mission in this chapter is to introduce you to a way to see how you are doing financially at any moment or period of time, compared to that same period last year. If you operate a small business, you must be aware of the value of such a program. Most small businesses rely on their accountant for this information, or you might have a program such as Quicken or Quickbooks. But, again if you rely on their canned reports, you might see how sales are doing, but you probably won't be able to determine what parts of the business are costing you more than others. If you rely on your accountant or bookkeeper, you'll likely be unaware if you're paying too much for inventory, or employees, or advertising. You'll know how much cash you have, but you won't know why it's too low, or what it will be next week.

Before I get into details, I would like to explain an income statement. It basically lists your income minus your expenses to get your profit. When you look at an accountant's income statement, it's not easy to figure out. In the system I'm about to explain, Incomes and expenses are broken down into categories and these categories can be real useful in your business decision making process. You, as a store owner, will have several categories of incomes including credit card, cash, finance company, taxable, non taxable, etc.
Your expenses are then further broken down. First, you have the amounts you spend on inventory. Then you have operating expenses and non-operating expenses. Non-operating expenses are not necessary for your business to operate. Examples are things like the owners auto, his exercise program, donations, organization dues, and similar. It's important when you are selling the business that these expenses are not part of the real measure of the costs. A new owner might not have or need these expenses. Your accountant includes only those that are deductible, but his job is to make you as poor as possible for tax purposes. Operating expenses are broken down into variable and fixed. Variable operating costs change as your income changes. If you have no customers, you'll have no variable operating costs. Finally, your regular operating costs can be broken down so you can see where you are spending your money. For example, your accountant puts all advertising expenses in one category. I break them down into newspaper,

billboards, TV, Radio, etc. The rest of this chapter should make this clearer.

An Indispensible Daily Management Tool

A Retail Profit and Loss Business Analysis Model

Note: After I wrote this Chapter, I reread it and thought to myself "Who in their right mind will read past the first few paragraphs?" If you are not bookkeeping oriented, this Chapter will read like an accounting textbook. If you ever took accounting in college, you'll know what I mean. I don't want you to try and read this Chapter and trash the whole book.

Before you read this Chapter, go to the Cost Comparison Report below. Look at the categories and how it is set up. Some of the categories will have to be changed to fit your particular business. Imagine if you could see this report every day to see how your business was doing and compare this month to the same month last year...or this year-to-date compared to last year. If that piques your interest, then you can read the Chapter, but keep in mind that most people will need help to set up this program. In my experience it was well worth it. (My apologies... this is the second Chapter where I had to write a note to prevent you from reading part of the Chapter and throwing it in the river.)

I've found this model to be extremely useful for small retail businesses with under 10 employees. The example I'm giving is the one I developed for my jewelry business. The same concept will work for almost all retail businesses. It will show you on a day-to-day, year-to-year or month-to-month comparison of how your business is performing. It is an instant estimate of profit and loss, and where your cash is going. It's actually one of the greatest information producing devices you can use in your business. Prior to this you had to wait until three months after the year is over for a 1040 form from your accountant....and who knows how to read that????? Even if you have a bookkeeper who maintains this model, you as a CEO will need to check this out on a daily basis.

This might work with Quickbooks, but I found Quickbooks very controlling. It was reluctant to let you set up your own categories. (I understand it has changed in recent years). I use regular Quicken Home and Business. Another advantage of this model is you don't have to enter transactions twice. As you print or electronically send your checks, the data are entered into the program at the same time. If this was just an analysis program, you would have to first write your checks and then enter the data in the separate analysis program.

The key to making this work is creating the correct categories for the Quicken Cash Flow Comparison report. Then, as you enter the checks and deposits under these categories, the report is basically automatic. My accountant doesn't want to see this report. In fact, all I have to do is email her a backup of the Quicken database and she creates a report on her computer that lays out the categories she uses to file my taxes. Since I started doing this, our bottom line results are close enough that I haven't been surprised when it comes time to send a check to the U.S. Treasury. I basically use the same categories as discussed in the cash flow model above, but I pay no attention to tax accounting rules. It was set up simply to analyze and watch everyday business.

The Quicken Cash Flow Comparison report is broken into two sections: Inflows and outflows. The key to this technique is the manipulation of sub-categories. The categories have to be entered in an outline hierarchy. Each time you enter a category in Quicken, it asks you what type of category it is and what category, if any, is it under. For example, first you enter a total income category under inflows. Then you enter a total sales and a cost of goods category as sub categories of total income. Then the Credit card sales category goes under the total sales category for example. The purchase inventory for stock category goes under the cost of goods category and you enter it as an income category despite the fact that it's an expense. It comes up as a negative, because cost of goods is subtracted from sales to form gross profit. As you examine the report this should make more sense:

Cash Flow Comparison

	Dec 2010	Dec 2011
Inflows		
1. Total Income		
A. Total Sales		
Credit Card Sales	64994.52	52557.92
Store Credit Sales	0.00	3469.32
Cash Sales	66076.04	47173.40
Tax Exempt Sales	2129.26	5117.00
Sales Tax Collected	*-8601.60*	*-5841.55*
Total Sales	124,598.22	102,476.09
B. Cost of Goods		
Payments on Acct Payable	*- 6975.81*	*- 2115.34*
Purchase I Special Orders	*-17925.04*	*-12,683.47*
Purchase Inventory Stock	*-9,196.36*	*-8506.04*
Purchase Inventory consign	*-33,708.46*	*-26,159.36*
Total cost of Goods	*-68,955.67*	*-50,978.21*
Total Income		
"Gross Profit "	55,642.55	51,497.88
Outflows		
Expenses		
1. Variable Operating Expenses		
B&O Taxes		
Commissions		
Credit Card Bank Debits	229.57	360.44
Outsourced Shop Work (repairs)	1,017.32	3746.47
Outsourced Watch Repair	434.75	0.00
Shop (Goldsmith) Expenses		
Shop Purchases	0.00	872.48
Shop Net Wages	3409.40	1990.88
Shop Withholding Taxes	861.20	763.84
Total Variable Operating Expenses	5,960.19	7734.11
2. Operating Expenses		
Basic Expenses		
Accounting Fees	0.00	0.00
Advertising Expenses		
Agency	2,700.00	0.00
Billboard	350.00	0.00
Direct Mail	0.00	0.00
Misc.		
Newspaper	1,000.00	1,000.00
Online	465.10	0.00
Radio	262.00	1,100.00
TV	4,350.00	0.00
Yellow Pages	124.85	126.30
Total Advertising	9,438.49	2561.30
Bank Charges		
Business Consulting Service	523.04	0.00

Business Travel expense		
Contract Labor	1,846.92	1347.27
Insurance	1,125.06	1,117.96
Interest	1,400.94	328.36
Misc Business Expense	1,204.77	1,634.05
Office		
Postage and Delivery	629.38	478.85
Rent	4,000.00	2,500.00
Supplies	986.78	1,186.39
Total Basic Expenses	21,155.38	11,154.39
Payroll Expenses		
Benefits Withheld From Income	0.00	162.31
Benefits Provided by employer	269.98	448.77
Wage Taxes		
Annual 940		
FUTA		
Monthly 941	1029.12	894.19
Quarterly Unemployment		
Quarterly Workmen's Comp		
State Employee Withholding	422.00	503.00
Wages – Net Paid		
Wages John	674.67	0.00
Wages Mary	967.81	1,018.72
Wages Irene	2,222.36	2,220.64
Wages Louie	586.17	683.98
Wages Tammy	27.98	0.00
Wages Jessica		84.37
Wages Natalie		
Total Wages net Paid	4,563.36	3923.34
Wages Owner		
Owner	0.00	1,398.33
Wages John Net	0.00	3,753.17
Total Wages owner	0.00	5,151.50
Total Payroll Expense	6,284.46	11,083.11
Tax, Business		
Misc Tax		
Property		
State Corporate Income Tax		
State Corporate Withholding		
Total Tax, Business	0.00	0.00
Utilities Business		
Computer Access	557.03	781.76
Electric	148.89	156.14
Garbage	14.70	15.20
Gas	42.05	175.00
Telephone	700.93	729.70
Water	254.88	0.00
Total Utilities Business	1,718.48	1,857.80
Total Operating Expenses	29,158.32	24,095.09
3. Non-Operating Expenses		
Auto		
Car Payment	455.76	432.36
Fuel	269.44	112.42
Insurance	192.80	179.99

Service		
Total Auto Expenses	918.00	724.77
Business Equipment		
Donations	956.70	1,016.89
Dues and Subscriptions	1,456.02	986.53
Executive Exercise Program	356.18	199.52
Total Non-Operating Expense	4,604.90	3,652.48
Total Expenses	39,723.41	35,481.68
Total Outflow		
Overall Total	15,919.14	16,016.20

Quicken lets you compare any two time periods. I am usually interested in month to date compared to the same period last year. Periodically I compared year to date this year and last. Now again I must emphasize the categories are not all tax deductible nor do they follow standard accounting practices. But as you examine the ways the categories are set up, you get an easy picture of cash flow and profit and loss. And, when you compare this year to last, it can get very enlightening.

I should note that I entered the cost of goods categories and the sales tax category as income categories . They show up as negatives and subtract from income to show a neat picture of cost of goods sold. Inventory on hand cannot be included here so you have to assume there was no appreciable change in inventory levels for the time periods analyzed. If you want to figure out the exact profit and loss for any time period, you have to add the beginning inventory on hand and subtract the ending inventory from the total purchases to determine gross profit for that time period. Then you subtract Variable and regular operating costs. (See the table at the end of this chapter). If you try to subtract non operating costs, you might be in trouble from a tax standpoint. For example, only part of your auto expenses are deductible and they may or may not allow you deductions for an executive exercise program. My accountant, to keep me safe usually adds those "expenses" to my personal income.

The advertising breakdowns are very informative as are the inventory purchases. Are you spending too much on stock vs. special orders, for example? When the bottom total is negative, you know why you have negative cash flow. All you have to do is look above to see which expenses are the most guilty and which can be dealt with next month.

I would recommend that you set up Quicken or any other accounting program with categories as demonstrated above. Every business will be different, so the categories might differ but it will be an extremely powerful business tool. If your system permits, it will pay to enter historical data. Even if you have a working accounting program, if you can't analyze your business it might pay to switch to Quicken. If you have difficulty setting up the categories, It would pay you to hire an accountant/bookkeeper to set it up for you. They might be able to improve on my categories.

You can also use this model as a cash flow monitor and projector. I set up an excel spreadsheet where I entered this report for each month of the year...with totals for year-to-date. It looked like a good idea, but I found that comparing any month with the same month last year was the most valuable use of the tool.

One more trick I use for channeling cash flow..... When I buy inventory, I'm usually given terms of one to six months. But, there's nothing worse than buying $10,000. worth of merchandise, selling it right away and then in six months having to pay for it in one lump sum.....especially if you replaced it three months ago and have another bill coming up for merchandise which is not yet sold. What I do, and my suppliers love this, is I set up automatic payments (in Quicken) weekly from right now through the next six months. For the $10,000 example, I would start paying $416 per week right now and in six months the merchandise is paid for whether it's sold or not. My total comfortable budget for buying inventory for stock might be $4000 per month, so I know I can afford to buy $25,000 each six months for inventory. On special orders, I pay them in full the instant they are paid for by the customer. These two tricks have kept my cash flow livable. This solves the problem of retailers who buy all their Christmas inventory in July for end of December payment. If they pay weekly from July through December, then they should have a pile of cash after a good December. If Christmas is bad, you should still have your head above water. If you wait until December to pay, and you sold some of the inventory before December, and December sales are mediocre, you could be in a lot of pain. This happened to me years ago, and I got out of trouble by explaining the problem to my suppliers and worked out a payment plan from January through March.

Another note on bookkeeping

In my experience, small business owners who use bookkeepers are wasting money and as a result are not as aware of the economic performance of their business as they should be. If Quicken is set up to print checks and to send them through Quicken Online Billpay and show the above report, bookkeeping is not a monstrous task. In the Jewelry business I write an average of three to five checks per day. Including the time I spend entering sales information, it amounts to 10 to 15 minutes. Included in that time, I use a payroll program and Quicken prints my payroll checks. It's the first thing I do each morning and after entering the day's transactions I look at the Cost Comparison Report. I know how much cash is in the bank accounts and I'm ready to start the day. If there are problems, I know about them first thing. By the way, it's also very important to do the bookkeeping every day for conservation of time reasons. If I waited and only entered weekly, it would take almost two hours... once per month and it would take a full day. Also, as I mentioned earlier, writing weekly checks makes dealing with cash flow almost fun.... Especially after years of being ruled by the cash flow monster.

If you want to calculate a real P&L summery for a given time period, you need to take the numbers from the cash flow comparison chart above, add the inventory on hand figures and put them in the following Excel chart:

P&L Calculator

Year 2012

Total Sales $624,808

Purchases	$308,267
Plus Accounts Payable Jan 1	$25,943
Minus Payments on Accts payable	$10,512
Plus Beginning Inventory Jan 1	$125,744
Minus Ending Inventory Dec 31	$138,231
Cost of Goods Sold	$311,211

Total Sales Minus Cost of Goods
   Sold = Gross Profit $313,597

Variable Operating Expenses $85,210

Fixed Operating Expenses
   Basic $96,995
   Payroll $101,542
   Taxes $3,722
   Utilities $20,807
     Total Fixed $223,066

     Total Operating Expenses $308,276

Gross Profit minus Variable Operating
  Expenses minus Fixed Operating Expenses
  = NET PROFIT $5321

Another Note: How to choose an accountant

   There are many accountants or CPA's in the
world. In my beginning years in business, I did my
own taxes and accounting as a single proprietor. As
business grew that became more complicated. I was
forced to hire an accountant. One of my good
customers was an accountant, so I hired him. He
was very expensive and he did my taxes each year.
On the day before my taxes were due, his junior
accountant handed me a 1040 form to file with the
IRS. It had a handy scotch taped arrow on where to
sign and instructions to send a check for $8000 to
the U.S. Treasury. It was a struggle to remain
conscious after seeing that. I asked "How could I
owe eight thousand dollars when I have a negative
cash flow and no money in in the bank account?" He
said I made a nice profit during the year. I looked at
the 1040 form and nothing there told me how I
managed to make a profit and have no money. I
asked for his help to find out and he really didn't
know either. All he could do was explain how he got
the numbers he put on the 1040 form.

   After that, I went to a different accountant who
was much cheaper. He also filled out my 1040 form.
Again I owed taxes and didn't know what I was
doing in the business that allowed me to have a
profit with no cash to show for it... Yes, I did know
my inventory was increasing each year, but was
clueless as to how to control it or how it affected my
profit.   This accountant couldn't help me either, but
at least he was cheaper.

It wasn't until I started working with business consultant Tom Bardeen that I started getting a handle on how to analyze the financial performance of the business. He showed me how big businesses use cash flow projections and how their accounting departments analyze performance. My challenge was to create a system that would work with a small family business using Quicken, instead of a mainframe computer analyzing millions of transactions.

Now I analyze my business with the charts above and I let my accountant convert all my real life categories into those textbook categories the IRS needs. Now our final P&L results are similar enough that I am never surprised when I owe taxes.... And when I do, I know exactly why.

So, if you want an accountant that can not only do your taxes but help you run your business, give them this chapter as a job interview. If they see the value of the Cost Comparison Report and are willing to help you set it up, I would say you should hire that accountant.

About The Author

John P. Kuehn, grew up in an entrepreneur family. My parents, after working various jobs, bought a small luncheonette in the 1950's. I grew up living, eating and eventually working in that restaurant. They built it from a small lunchroom to a three-store restaurant chain. After that upbringing, I was too smart to work in a restaurant....I went to school and became a college professor. I wasn't going to spend 70 hours a week working in a hot kitchen. However, after only six years as a successful professor, I began to resent office politics...I began to resent getting the same salary raises as everyone else, even though I felt we should be paid based on productivity, not on tenure. I also wanted to be in a situation where if the boss was in a bad mood, I wouldn't be affected.

I decided to start a part-time side business of some kind. The gene was emerging. It took two years of research to figure out what type of business to start and how to do it without a large investment. I decided to open a fine jewelry upstairs office in our downtown. I took the courses (I was very experienced in taking courses) to become a Gemologist and in my office I did jewelry appraisals and sold jewelry out of catalogs. Since I had no overhead, I was able to under price any jewelry store within 60 miles. I was open two weekday evenings and Saturdays. My initial investment was $700.00 including four diamond rings and a $20 grand opening ad in the local newspaper

It took five years of only word-of-mouth advertising and I was finally making enough to take some spending money home. I was still teaching economics. Three years later, I was making enough in that office to leave the University and go 100 percent into business. I opened a small downtown storefront and grew into a larger storefront. Almost all of my money was tied up in inventory. I was making a living...loving it...but I was working sixty hours a week.... sound familiar?

Business was ongoing for fifteen or so years and nothing much was changing. I thought I knew about marketing because I taught the course years ago, but business was just carrying on at a slow steady pace with no major growth, except in the form of net worth... inventory I hadn't sold. I realized that change was necessary, but didn't know how or what to change into.

I needed help and made dozens of phone calls...there was very little online in those days. Through a best selling book, The E-Myth Revisited, by Michael Gerber, I found The E-Myth Company. They assigned me a business coach, Thomas O. Bardeen... After asking me a dozen or so questions on my business, he asked me what would happen if I doubled my prices.... I estimated I would lose half of my clientele... my gross sales would go down fifty percent. He said "O.K, go and do the math. Assume you doubled your prices and half your clientele left". It took two hours with my rudimentary bookkeeping system and a calculator....I couldn't believe the results... My gross sales were cut in half but my net profit went up by a factor of FIVE!!!!!! I made five times more money with half the work. Tom then explained that doubling your prices is an unrealistic approach, but the exercise pointed out that I wasn't attracting the right target market. If I committed to the business development course, he could help me achieve the increase in net profit without losing half of my clientele... I hired him!!!! And in so doing became a business consultant myself.

My gross sales went from $500,000 to $988,000 in the three years following the introduction of the practices, rules and procedures I learned.... And with no significant investment.

I have recently semi-retired from the jewelry business and turned it over to my daughters.... I wanted to teach them the course, but they watched the transformation as it occurred, and Dad's don't always know everything.... I spend about three hours a week tending to their needs and I have been mentoring small business and walking nine holes of golf almost every day.

John earned his B.S. Degree from Rutgers University in 1964, a Master's from the University of Vermont in 1965 and a PhD from the University of Tennessee in 1969. He taught at West Virginia University from 1969 through 1984.

www.yourbusinessdoc.com

john@yourbusinessdoc.com

www.ingramcontent.com/pod-product-compliance
Lightning Source LLC
Chambersburg PA
CBHW051503170526
45166CB00001B/364